The Merrill Studies
in
The Marble Faun

CHARLES E. MERRILL STUDIES

Under the General Editorship of
Matthew J. Bruccoli and Joseph Katz

The Merrill Studies
in
The Marble Faun

Compiled by

David B. Kesterson
North Texas State University

Charles E. Merrill Publishing Company
A Bell & Howell Company
Columbus, Ohio

Preface

"The idea keeps recurring to me of writing a little Romance about the Faun of Praxiteles," Hawthorne confided to his journal on April 30, 1858, in only one of several references he made to the germinal seeds of his new romance. The fragmentary English romance he had been working on while in Italy—*The Ancestral Footstep*—was put aside, and in Florence in the summer of 1858 Hawthorne began sketching out the "Romance of Monte Beni." Three drafts and a year and a half later the book appeared in late February, 1860, as *Transformation* in England and in early March as *The Marble Faun* in America. Eight years had elapsed since the publication of Hawthorne's last novel, *The Blithedale Romance*, and the close of his most productive creative period.

Public reaction to *The Marble Faun* was highly favorable both in England and America, and reviews were universally complimentary. The only major objection to the novel was the lack of a concrete ending, a criticism which Hawthorne chose to offset somewhat by adding a slightly revealing epilogue to the second edition (still insisting, of course, that vagueness in the romance is one of its essential properties).

Since the later nineteenth century, criticism of *The Marble Faun* has taken two major directions. The novel has been praised by many as being the most ambitious of Hawthorne's works, especially because of its rich texture, the mature thematic development, and the complex interplay of characters. Hawthorne's handling of the problems of good and evil, original sin, and the idea of the Fortunate Fall reaches a masterful culmination here, asserts this

v

group of readers. On the other hand, detractors have pointed out in *The Marble Faun* signs of Hawthorne's disintegration as artist: the dominant use of Italian background which gives the book something of a guidebook aura, the slavish "borrowings," as they have been called, from the Italian journals, the rather weak resolution of the Fortunate Fall theme, and the failure to draw Hilda convincingly.

Hawthorne's own reactions to *The Marble Faun* were frequently ambivalent, but his final impression was one of esteem. He seemed to grow more appreciative of its merits as time went by. He remarked to friend James T. Fields that the book was by far "the best" work he had done and to William D. Ticknor that he had "never thought or felt more deeply, or taken more pains" than when writing *The Marble Faun*. Modern critics appear to be leaning in Hawthorne's own direction, for most current views are favorable. Even those critics who see the novel as a failure in some respects, generally express admiration of its design and fabric and cull out much to praise. One could say it is only inevitable that in time *The Marble Faun* has come into its own as a novel to be reread, taught, and discussed—but it seems to me rather that its richness of texture and depth of setting, theme, and characterization are themselves responsible for bringing the novel to the critical attention it deserves.

In selecting the essays in this book, I have looked both for excellence and range of major subjects treated. From the early reviews and critical voices down to the present, the essays are arranged to treat matters of the Italian setting and sources, structure and technique, theme, characterization, and general evaluation and interpretation.

D. B. K.

Contents

1. Early Reviews and Criticism

2. Twentieth-Century Views

1. Early Reviews and Criticism

James Russell Lowell

The Marble Faun.
A Romance of Monte Beni

It is, we believe, more than thirty years since Mr. Hawthorne's
first appearance as an author; it is twenty-three since he gave his
first collection of "Twice-told Tales" to the world. His works have
received that surest warranty of genius and originality in the widening of their appreciation downward from a small circle of refined
admirers and critics, till it embraced the whole community of readers. With just enough encouragement to confirm his faith in his
own powers, those powers had time to ripen and toughen themselves before the gales of popularity could twist them from the
balance of a healthy and normal development. Happy the author
whose earliest works are read and understood by the lustre thrown
back upon them from his latest! for then we receive the impression
of continuity and cumulation of power, of peculiarity deepening
to individuality, of promise more than justified in the keeping:
unhappy, whose autumn shows only the aftermath and rowen of
an earlier harvest, whose would-be replenishments are but thin
dilutions of his fame!

The nineteenth century has produced no more purely original
writer than Mr. Hawthorne. A shallow criticism has sometimes
fancied a resemblance between him and Poe. But it seems to us
that the difference between them is the immeasurable one between
talent carried to its ultimate, and genius,—between a masterly
adaptation of the world of sense and appearance to the purposes
of Art, and a so thorough conception of the world of moral realities
that Art becomes the interpreter of something profounder than
herself. In this respect it is not extravagant to say that Hawthorne
has something of kindred with Shakspeare. But that breadth of
nature which made Shakspeare incapable of alienation from common human nature and actual life is wanting to Hawthorne. He is
rather a denizen than a citizen of what men call the world. We are
conscious of a certain remoteness in his writings, as in those of
Donne, but with such a difference that we should call the one
super- and the other subter-sensual. Hawthorne is psychological
and metaphysical. Had he been born without the poetic imagina-

Reprinted from *Atlantic Monthly,* V (April, 1860), 509–10.

tion, he would have written treatises on the Origin of Evil. He does not draw characters, but rather conceives them and then shows them acted upon by crime, passion, or circumstance, as if the element of Fate were as present to his imagination as to that of a Greek dramatist. Helen we know, and Antigone, and Benedick, and Falstaff, and Miranda, and Parson Adams, and Major Pendennis,—these people have walked on pavements or looked out of club-room windows; but what are these idiosyncrasies into which Mr. Hawthorne has breathed a necromantic life, and which he has endowed with the forms and attributes of men? And yet, grant him his premises, that is, let him once get his morbid tendency, whether inherited or the result of special experience, either incarnated as a new man or usurping all the faculties of one already in the flesh, and it is marvelous how subtilely and with what truth to as much of human nature as is included in a diseased consciousness he traces all the finest nerves of impulse and motive, how he compels every trivial circumstance into an accomplice of his art, and makes the sky flame with foreboding or the landscape chill and darken with remorse. It is impossible to think of Hawthorne without at the same time thinking of the few great masters of imaginative composition; his works, only not abstract because he has the genius to make them ideal, belong not specially to our clime or generation; it is their moral purpose alone, and perhaps their sadness, that mark him as the son of New England and the Puritans.

It is commonly true of Hawthorne's romances that the interest centres in one strongly defined protagonist, to whom the other characters are accessory and subordinate,—perhaps we should rather say a ruling Idea, of which all the characters are fragmentary embodiments. They remind us of a symphony of Beethoven's, in which, though there be variety of parts, yet all are infused with the dominant motive, and heighten its impression by hints and faraway suggestions at the most unexpected moment. As in Rome the obelisks are placed at points toward which several streets converge, so in Mr. Hawthorne's stories the actors and incidents seem but vistas through which we see the moral from different points of view,—a moral pointing skyward always, but inscribed with hieroglyphs mysteriously suggestive, whose incitement to conjecture, while they baffle it, we prefer to any prosaic solution.

Nothing could be more original or imaginative than the conception of the character of Donatello in Mr. Hawthorne's new romance. His likeness to the lovely statue of Praxiteles, his happy

animal temperament, and the dim legend of his pedigree are combined with wonderful art to reconcile us to the notion of a Greek
myth embodied in an Italian of the nineteenth century; and when
at length a soul is created in this primeval pagan, this child of
earth, this creature of mere instinct, awakened through sin to a
conception of the necessity of atonement, we feel, that, while we
looked to be entertained with the airiest of fictions, we were dealing
with the most august truths of psychology, with the most pregnant
facts of modern history, and studying a profound parable of the
development of the Christian Idea.

Everything suffers a sea-change in the depths of Mr. Hawthorne's mind, gets rimmed with an impalpable fringe of melancholy moss, and there is a tone of sadness in this book as in the
rest, but it does not leave us sad. In a series of remarkable and
characteristic works, it is perhaps the most remarkable and characteristic. If you had picked up and read a stray leaf of it anywhere, you would have exclaimed, "Hawthorne!"

The book is steeped in Italian atmosphere. There are many
landscapes in it full of breadth and power, and criticisms of pictures and statues always delicate, often profound. In the Preface,
Mr. Hawthorne pays a well-deserved tribute of admiration to several of our sculptors, especially to Story and Akers. The hearty
enthusiasm with which he elsewhere speaks of the former artist's
"Cleopatra" is no surprise to Mr. Story's friends at home, though
hardly less gratifying to them than it must be to the sculptor
himself.

E. P. Whipple

[Review of *The Marble Faun*]

. . . Eight years have passed since "The Blithedale Romance"
was written, and during nearly the whole of this period Hawthorne
has resided abroad. "The Marble Faun," which must, on the whole,

Reprinted from *Atlantic Monthly*, V (May, 1860), 620–22.

be considered the greatest of his works, proves that his genius has widened and deepened in this interval, without any alteration or modification of its characteristic merits and characteristic defects. The most obvious excellence of the work is the vivid truthfulness of its descriptions of Italian life, manners, and scenery; and, considered merely as a record of a tour in Italy, it is of great interest and attractiveness. The opinions on Art, and the special criticisms on the masterpieces of architecture, sculpture, and painting, also possess a value of their own. The story might have been told, and the characters fully represented, in one-third of the space devoted to them, yet description and narration are so artfully combined that each assists to give interest to the other. Hawthorne is one of those true observers who concentrate in observation every power of their minds. He has accurate sight and piercing insight. When he modifies either the form or the spirit of the objects he describes, he does it either by viewing them through the medium of an imagined mind or by obeying associations which they themselves suggest. We might quote from the descriptive portions of the work a hundred pages, at least, which would demonstrate how closely accurate observation is connected with the highest powers of the intellect and imagination.

The style of the book is perfect of its kind, and, if Hawthorne had written nothing else, would entitle him to rank among the great masters of English composition. Walter Savage Landor is reported to have said of an author whom he knew in his youth, "My friend wrote excellent English, a language now obsolete." Had "The Marble Faun" appeared before he uttered this sarcasm, the wit of the remark would have been pointless. Hawthorne not only writes English, but the sweetest, simplest, and clearest English that ever has been made the vehicle of equal depth, variety, and subtilty of thought and emotion. His mind is reflected in his style as a face is reflected in a mirror; and the latter does not give back its image with less appearance of effort than the former. His excellence consists not so much in using common words as in making common words express uncommon things. Swift, Addison, Goldsmith, not to mention others, wrote with as much simplicity; but the style of neither embodies an individuality so complex, passions so strange and intense, sentiments so fantastic and preternatural, thoughts so profound and delicate, and imaginations so remote from the recognized limits of the ideal, as find an orderly outlet in the pure English of Hawthorne. He has hardly a word to which Mrs. Trimmer would primly object, hardly a sentence which would call forth

the frosty anathema of Blair, Hurd, Kames, or Whately, and yet
he contrives to embody in his simple style qualities which would
almost excuse the verbal extravagances of Carlyle.

In regard to the characterization and plot of "The Marble Faun,"
there is room for widely varying opinions. Hilda, Miriam, and
Donatello will be generally received as superior in power and depth
to any of Hawthorne's previous creations of character; Donatello,
especially, must be considered one of the most original and exquisite conceptions in the whole range of romance; but the story
in which they appear will seem to many an unsolved puzzle, and
even the tolerant and interpretative "gentle reader" will be
troubled with the unsatisfactory conclusion. It is justifiable for a
romancer to sting the curiosity of his readers with a mystery, only
on the implied obligation to explain it at last; but this story begins
in mystery only to end in mist. The suggestive faculty is tor-
mented rather than genially excited, and in the end is left a prey
to doubts. The central idea of the story, the necessity of sin to
convert such a creature as Donatello into a moral being, is also not
happily illustrated in the leading event. When Donatello kills the
wretch who malignantly dogs the steps of Miriam, all readers
think that Donatello committed no sin at all; and the reason is,
that Hawthorne has deprived the persecutor of Miriam of all
human attributes, made him an allegorical representation of one
of the most fiendish forms of unmixed evil, so that we welcome his
destruction with something of the same feeling with which, in
following the allegory of Spenser or Bunyan, we rejoice in the
hero's victory over the Blatant Beast or Giant Despair. Con-
ceding, however, that Donatello's act was murder, and not "justifiable homicide," we are still not sure that the author's conception
of his nature and of the change caused in his nature by that act,
are carried out with a felicity corresponding to the original
conception.

In the first volume, and in the early part of the second, the
author's hold on his design is comparatively firm, but it somewhat relaxes as he proceeds, and in the end it seems almost to
escape from his grasp. Few can be satisfied with the concluding
chapters, for the reason that nothing is really concluded. We are
willing to follow the ingenious processes of Calhoun's deductive
logic, because we are sure, that, however severely they task the
faculty of attention, they will lead to some positive result; but
Hawthorne's logic of events leaves us in the end bewildered in a
labyrinth of guesses. The book is, on the whole, such a great book,
that its defects are felt with all the more force....

Henry James

[*The Marble Faun*]

... It is an odd fact that in the two countries the book came out under different titles. The title that the author had bestowed upon it did not satisfy the English publishers, who requested him to provide it with another; so that it is only in America that the work bears the name of *The Marble Faun*. Hawthorne's choice of this appellation is, by the way, rather singular, for it completely fails to characterise the story, the subject of which is the living faun, the faun of flesh and blood, the unfortunate Donatello. His marble counterpart is mentioned only in the opening chapter. On the other hand, Hawthorne complained that *Transformation* "gives one the idea of Harlequin in a pantomine." Under either name, however, the book was a great success, and it has probably become the most popular of Hawthorne's four novels. It is part of the intellectual equipment of the Anglo-Saxon visitor to Rome, and is read by every English-speaking traveller who arrives there, who has been there, or who expects to go.

It has a great deal of beauty, of interest and grace; but it has, to my sense, a slighter value than its companions, and I am far from regarding it as the masterpiece of the author, a position to which we sometimes hear it assigned. The subject is admirable, and so are many of the details; but the whole thing is less simple and complete than either of the three tales of American life, and Hawthorne forfeited a precious advantage in ceasing to tread his native soil. Half the virtue of *The Scarlet Letter* and *The House of the Seven Gables* is in their local quality; they are impregnated with the New England air. It is very true that Hawthorne had no pretension to portray actualities, and to cultivate that literal exactitude which is now the fashion. Had this been the case, he would probably have made a still graver mistake in transporting the scene of his story to a country which he knew only superficially. His tales all go on more or less "in the vague," as the French say, and of course the vague may as well be placed in Tuscany as in Massachusetts. It may also very well be urged in Hawthorne's favour here, that in *Transformation* he has attempted to deal with actualities more than he did in either of his earlier novels. He has

Reprinted from *Hawthorne* (New York: Harper & Brothers, 1880), pp. 159–64.

7

described the streets and monuments of Rome with a closeness which forms no part of his reference to those of Boston and Salem. But for all this he incurs that penalty of seeming factitious and unauthoritative, which is always the result of an artist's attempt to project himself into an atmosphere in which he has not a transmitted and inherited property. An English or a German writer (I put poets aside) may love Italy well enough, and know her well enough, to write delightful fictions about her; the thing has often been done. But the productions in question will, as novels, always have about them something second-rate and imperfect. There is in *Transformation* enough beautiful perception of the interesting character of Rome, enough rich and eloquent expression of it, to save the book, if the book could be saved; but the style, what the French call the *genre*, is an inferior one, and the thing remains a charming romance with intrinsic weaknesses.

Allowing for this, however, some of the finest pages in all Hawthorne are to be found in it. The subject, as I have said, is a particularly happy one, and there is a great deal of interest in the simple combination and opposition of the four actors. It is noticeable that, in spite of the considerable length of the story, there are no accessory figures; Donatello and Miriam, Kenyon and Hilda exclusively occupy the scene. This is the more noticeable as the scene is very large, and the great Roman background is constantly presented to us. The relations of these four people are full of that moral picturesqueness which Hawthorne was always looking for; he found it in perfection in the history of Donatello. As I have said, the novel is the most popular of his works, and every one will remember the figure of the simple, joyous, sensuous young Italian, who is not so much a man as a child, and not so much a child as a charming, innocent animal, and how he is brought to self-knowledge, and to a miserable conscious manhood, by the commission of a crime. Donatello is rather vague and impalpable; he says too little in the book, shows himself too little, and falls short, I think, of being a creation. But he is enough of a creation to make us enter into the situation, and the whole history of his rise, or fall, whichever one chooses to call it—his tasting of the tree of knowledge, and finding existence complicated with a regret—is unfolded with a thousand ingenious and exquisite touches. Of course, to make the interest complete, there is a woman in the affair; and Hawthorne has done few things more beautiful than the picture of the unequal complicity of guilt between his immature and dimly-puzzled hero, with his clinging, unquestioning, unexacting devotion, and the dark, powerful, more widely-seeing feminine nature of Miriam. Deeply touching is the representation of the manner in which these two essentially different persons—the woman intelligent, passionate, acquainted with life, and with a tragic element in her own career; the youth ignorant, gentle, unworldly, brightly and harmlessly natural—are equalised and bound together by their common secret, which insulates them, morally, from the rest of mankind. The character of Hilda has always struck me as an admirable invention—one of those things that mark the man of genius. It needed a man of genius and of Hawthorne's imaginative delicacy, to feel the propriety of such a figure as Hilda's, and to perceive the relief it would both give and borrow. This pure and somewhat rigid New England girl, following the vocation of a copyist of pictures in Rome, unacquainted with evil and untouched by impurity, has been accidentally the witness, unknown and unsuspected, of the dark deed by which her friends, Miriam and Donatello, are knit together. This is *her* revelation of evil, her loss of perfect innocence. She has done no wrong, and yet wrong-doing has become a part of her experience, and she carries the weight of her detested knowledge upon her heart. She carries it a long time, saddened and oppressed by it, till at last she can bear it no longer. If I have called the whole idea of the presence and effect of Hilda in the story a trait of genius, the purest touch of inspiration is the episode in which the poor girl deposits her burden. She has passed the whole lonely summer in Rome; and one day, at the end of it, finding herself in St. Peter's, she enters a confessional, strenuous daughter of the Puritans as she is, and pours out her dark knowledge into the bosom of the church— then comes away with her conscience lightened, not a whit the less a Puritan than before. If the book contained nothing else noteworthy but this admirable scene, and the pages describing the murder committed by Donatello under Miriam's eyes, and the ecstatic wandering, afterwards, of the guilty couple through the "blood-stained streets of Rome," it would still deserve to rank high among the imaginative productions of our day.

Like all of Hawthorne's things, it contains a great many light threads of symbolism, which shimmer in the texture of the tale, but which are apt to break and remain in our fingers if we attempt to handle them. These things are part of Hawthorne's very manner—almost, as one might say, of his vocabulary; they belong much more to the surface of his work than to its stronger interest.

The fault of *Transformation* is that the element of the unreal is pushed too far, and that the book is neither positively of one category nor of another. His "moonshiny romance," he calls it in a letter; and, in truth, the lunar element is a little too pervasive. The action wavers between the streets of Rome, whose literal features the author perpetually sketches, and a vague realm of fancy, in which quite a different verisimilitude prevails. This is the trouble with Donatello himself. His companions are intended to be real— if they fail to be so, it is not for want of intention; whereas he is intended to be real or not, as you please. He is of a different substance from them; it is as if a painter, in composing a picture, should try to give you an impression of one of his figures by a strain of music. The idea of the modern faun was a charming one; but I think it a pity that the author should not have made him more definitely modern, without reverting so much to his mythological properties and antecedents, which are very gracefully touched upon, but which belong to the region of picturesque conceits, much more than to that of real psychology. Among the young Italians of to-day there are still plenty of models for such an image as Hawthorne appears to have wished to present in the easy and natural Donatello. And since I am speaking critically, I may go on to say that the art of narration, in *Transformation*, seems to me more at fault than in the author's other novels. The story straggles and wanders, is dropped and taken up again, and towards the close lapses into an almost fatal vagueness.

Anthony Trollope

The Genius of
Nathaniel Hawthorne

... In speaking of "The Marble Faun," as I will call the story, I hardly know whether, as a just critic, to speak first of its faults or

Reprinted from *North American Review*, CXXIX (September, 1879), 220–22.

of its virtues. As one always likes to keep the sweetest bits for the end of the banquet, I will give priority of place to my caviling. The great fault of the book lies in the absence of arranged plot. The author, in giving the form of a novel to the beautiful pictures and images which his fancy has enabled him to draw, and in describing Rome and Italian scenes as few others have described them, has in fact been too idle to carry out his own purpose of constructing a tale. We will grant that a novelist may be natural or supernatural. Let us grant, for the occasion, that the latter manner, if well handled, is the better and the more efficacious. And we must grant also that he who soars into the supernatural need not bind himself by any of the ordinary trammels of life. His men may fly, his birds may speak. His women may make angelic music without instruments. His cherubs may sit at the piano. This wide latitude, while its adequate management is much too difficult for ordinary hands, gives facility for the working of a plot. But there must be some plot, some arrangement of circumstances, with an intelligible conclusion, or the reader will not be satisfied. If, then, a ghost, who,—or shall I say which?—is made on all occasions to act as a *Deus ex machina*, and to create and to solve every interest, we should know something of the ghost's antecedents, something of the causes which have induced him, or it, to meddle in the matter under discussion. The ghost of Hamlet's father had a manifest object, and the ghost of Banquo a recognized cause. In "The Marble Faun" there is no ghost, but the heroine of the story is driven to connive at murder, and the hero to commit murder, by the disagreeable intrusion of a personage whose *raison d'être* is left altogether in the dark. "The gentle reader," says our author as he ends his narrative, "would not thank us for one of those minute elucidations which are so tedious and after all so unsatisfactory in clearing up the romantic mysteries of a story." There our author is, I think, in error. His readers will hardly be so gentle as not to require from him some explanation of the causes which have produced the romantic details to which they have given their attention, and will be inclined to say that it should have been the author's business to give an explanation neither tedious nor unsatisfactory. The critic is disposed to think that Hawthorne, as he continued his narrative, postponed his plot till it was too late, and then escaped from his difficulty by the ingenious excuse above given. As a writer of novels, I am bound to say that the excuse can not be altogether accepted.

But the fault, when once admitted, may be well pardoned on

account of the beauty of the narrative. There are four persons,—
or five, including the mysterious intruder who is only, I think, seen
and never heard, but who is thrown down the Tarpeian rock and
murdered. Three of them are artists,—a lady named Miriam, who
is haunted by the mysterious one and is an assenting party to his
murder; another lady named Hilda, an American from New England, who lives alone in a tower surrounded by doves; and a
sculptor, one Kenyon, also from the States, who is in love with
Hilda. The fourth person is the Faun, as to whom the reader is left
in doubt whether he be man or Satyr,—human, or half god half
animal. As to this doubt the critic makes no complaint. The author
was within his right in creating a creature partaking of these different attributes, and it has to be acknowledged on his behalf that
the mystery which he has thrown over this offspring of his brain has
been handled by him, a writer of prose, not only with profound
skill but with true poetic feeling. This faun, who is Count of Monte
Beni,—be he most god, or man, or beast; let him have come from
the hills and the woods and the brooks like a Satyr of old, or as any
other count from his noble ancestors and ancestral towers,—attaches himself to Miriam, as a dog does to a man, not with an expressed human love in which there is a longing for kisses and a hope
for marriage, but with a devotion half doglike as I have said, but
in its other half godlike and heavenly pure. He scampers round her
in his joy, and is made happy simply by her presence, her influence,
and her breath. He is happy, except when the intruder intrudes,
and then his jealousy is that as of a dog against an intruding hound.
There comes a moment in which the intrusion of the intruder is
unbearable. Then he looks into Miriam's eyes, and, obtaining the
assent for which he seeks, he hurls the intruder down the Tarpeian
rock into eternity. After that the light-hearted creature, overwhelmed by the weight of his sin, becomes miserable, despondent,
and unable to bear the presence of her who had so lately been all
the world to him. In the end light-hearted joy returns to him; but
the reason for this second change is not so apparent.

The lives of Kenyon and Hilda are more commonplace, but,
though they are commonplace between man and woman, the manner in which they are told is very beautiful. She is intended to represent perfect innocence, and he manly honesty. The two characters are well conceived and admirably expressed.

In "The Marble Faun," as in all Hawthorne's tales written after
"The Scarlet Letter," the reader must look rather for a series of
pictures than for a novel. It would, perhaps, almost be well that a

fastidious reader should cease to read when he comes within that border, toward the end, in which it might be natural to expect that the strings of a story should be gathered together and tied into an intelligible knot. This would be peculiarly desirable in regard to "The Marble Faun," in which the delight of that fastidious reader, as derived from pictures of character and scenery, will be so extreme that it should not be marred by a sense of failure in other respects.

In speaking of this work in conjunction with Hawthorne's former tales, I should be wrong not to mention the wonderful change which he effected in his own manner of writing when he had traveled out from Massachusetts into Italy. As every word in his earlier volumes savors of New England, so in "The Marble Faun" is the flavor entirely that of Rome and of Italian scenery. His receptive imagination took an impress from what was around him, and then gave it forth again with that wonderful power of expression which belonged to him. Many modern writers have sought to give an interest to their writings by what is called local coloring; but it will too often happen that the reader is made to see the laying on of the colors. In Hawthorne's Roman chronicle the tone of the telling is just as natural,—seems to belong as peculiarly to the author,—as it does with "The Scarlet Letter" or "The House of the Seven Gables."

Elia W. Peattie

On a Blank Leaf in "The Marble Faun"

I cannot tell why these sad oaken groves
Should bring to mind the gay and mystic glades
    Where Donatello danced;
I dare not guess, while my eye, restless, roves

Reprinted from *The Century Magazine,* XLII (October, 1891), 847.

This stormy lake, and daylight fades,
  Why I have chanced
To dream of some bright pool where shimmering lie
The tender shadows of the Tuscan sky.

I sing no songs that are not grave and old!
Why should the merry Tuscan haunt my dreams?
    How light of foot was he!—
The sky is dun, the wind is wet and cold,
Dead, drear, and dull each swelling sand-dune seems;
    What then to me
Is all this wild, midsummer fantasy,
This mellow, mad, and witching mockery?

'T was something in your eyes—I swear it, friend,
For you seemed part of stream, and wood, and field.
    I've watched your soul grow young!
On days of sun, into the joy you blend,
On days of shade, into the grief you yield;
    The balance hung
On perfect scale, which lightest touch might sway,
The perfect glass reflect the palest morning ray.

Oh, learn no wisdom, for that may bring grief;
And love no woman, for 't will sure bring pain;
    Be Donatello still!
Believe me, friend, this learning is a thief,
And where it thrives the simple joys are slain.
    Ah, drink your fill
Of sky and hill, of sun and wind and sea;
Be thou my faun, but I no Miriam to thee.

2. Twentieth-Century Views

Gary J. Scrimgeour

The Marble Faun:
Hawthorne's Faery Land

In the years following Hawthorne's death, *The Marble Faun* was his most widely read romance. Its popularity, especially in the illustrated Tauchnitz edition, was due largely to its Italian setting. As Henry James wrote in 1879, it became "part of the intellectual equipment of the Anglo-Saxon visitor to Rome, and is read by every English-speaking traveller who arrives there, who has been there, or who expects to go." [1] Critics, however, have not usually shared the readers' enjoyment of the Italian setting. James thought that Hawthorne "forfeited a precious advantage in ceasing to tread his native soil," and sixty years later F. O. Matthiessen agreed that "the backdrops of scenery impede the action." [2] But in recent criticism there have been signs that the Italianateness of *The Marble Faun* is gaining in esteem, and my own suggestion is that Hawthorne's choice of locale for his story and the detail of his exploitation of that locale are absolutely essential to his romance—that in fact we cannot understand the work unless we see it, in Hawthorne's own terms, as a "tapestry . . . woven with the best of the artist's skill, and cunningly arranged with a view to the harmonious exhibition of its colors." [3]

The Preface to *The Marble Faun* shows that Hawthorne knew exactly why he selected Italy as his locale. We are all a trifle bored by the oft-quoted words, and perhaps made uneasy by their jocularity, so that we are in danger of forgetting that they are, in fact, an explicit and almost literal statement of the author's purposes:

Italy, as the site of his Romance, was chiefly valuable to [the author] as affording a sort of poetic or fairy precinct, where actu-

Reprinted from *American Literature,* XXXVI (November, 1964), 271–87, with permission of the Duke University Press and the author.

[1] *Hawthorne* (London, 1879), p. 165. The Tauchnitz edition first appeared in 1860, and contained 54 mounted photographs. Subsequent American and English editions were also illustrated.

[2] James, p. 165; Matthiessen, *American Renaissance* (New York, 1941), p. 275.

[3] *The Marble Faun, The Complete Works of Nathaniel Hawthorne* (Cambridge, Mass., 1883), VI, 514.

alities would not be so terribly insisted upon as they are, and must needs be, in America. No author, without a trial, can conceive of the difficulty of writing a romance about a country where there is no shadow, no antiquity, no mystery, no picturesque and gloomy wrong, nor anything but a commonplace prosperity, in broad and simple daylight, as is happily the case with my dear native land. It will be very long, I trust, before romance-writers may find congenial and easily handled themes, either in the annals of our stalwart republic, or in any characteristic and probable events of our individual lives. Romance and poetry, ivy, lichens, and wallflowers, need ruin to make them grow.

Hawthorne is again seeking the world he had tried to create in the American romances: "Faery Land, so like the real world, that, in a suitable remoteness, one cannot well tell the difference, but with an atmosphere of strange enchantment, beheld through which the inhabitants have a propriety of their own" (Preface to *The Blithedale Romance*). In Italy he found materials that made his task easier than it had been. He found objects "antique, pictorial and statuesque" which offered themselves to his peculiarly symbolic mind; he found a society of individuals with "a propriety of their own" that makes their preoccupation with his themes "characteristic and probable"; he found a land naturally invested with an atmosphere half-mysterious but definitely real; and he found a world in which time—eternity, the past, the present—was manifest and observable.[4]

The most usual targets of criticism are the art objects and guidebook sights which Hawthorne could not, he says, "find it in his heart to cancel," though he was "surprised" at the frequency with which they appear. I suspect his attitude was more positive than he admits. There is little doubt that he deliberately selected Italy's most widely publicized monuments, sculptures, and paintings for inclusion, and we can understand his reasoning if we see the problem he faced in the American romances. There, to create his romantic atmosphere, he had to take objects that were stolidly actual and invest them with connotations which, in most cases, they did not already have. In *The Marble Faun*, on the other hand,

---

[4] Three other useful studies of the Italian material are Darrel Abel, "A Masque of Love and Death," *University of Toronto Quarterly*, XXIII, 9–25 (Oct., 1953); James K. Folsom, "The Principle of Multiplicity in Hawthorne's Fiction," unpublished dissertation (Princeton University, 1959); Arlin Turner, *Nathaniel Hawthorne: An Introduction and Interpretation* (New York, 1961).

in choosing the most famous, the most conventional, the most frequently discussed objects, he was choosing things that were already both actual and romantic, that, because of their traditional connotations, existed in both the real world and Faery Land. Thus Italy resolved his recurring dilemma between novel and romance by enabling him simply to copy observations recorded in his journals. To make the same point another way, Hawthorne's choice of art objects is banal from the viewpoint of art but exceptionally fit for communication with the reader.

Hawthorne suffered from a weakness of aesthetic taste that was as apparent to him as it is to us. He paid no serious attention to painting until he visited the Manchester Arts Exhibition in 1857, when he was fifty-three years old. Then and during their later visits to the Italian galleries, his wife Sophia was the force behind his interest and the main source of his information. On April 12, 1858, he recorded in his journal that "all this Greek beauty has done something towards refining me, though I am still, however, a very sturdy Goth." [5] And of his visit to Florence in the summer of the same year, his son Julian wrote:

> In fact, he had not got so far in his pictorial training as to analyze the composition of a picture; he observed the workmanship, whether it were finished or rough, and the colors, whether they were brilliant or dull; but, for the rest, he accepted the work as it was, and either liked it or not, as if it were pleasant or a disagreeable person. Of technicalities,—difficulties overcome, harmony of lines, and so forth,—he had no explicit knowledge.... All that concerned him was the sentiment which the artist had meant to express; the means and method were comparatively unimportant.[6]

This, we may say, is philistinism. But it is a philistinism which most of his readers shared, and through it Hawthorne established the community of interest which enabled him to transmit directly to them the material which interested him, rather than irrelevant art criticism. Guilty or not of provincialism himself, he used the provincialism of his readers to create his real-unreal world.

The critiques of art in *The Marble Faun*, far from being irrelevant, are used for burdens previously shouldered by more mundane

---

[5] *Passages from the French and Italian Notebooks, Complete Works*, X, 159.
[6] *Nathaniel Hawthorne and His Wife* (Boston, 1885), II, 193. Julian suggests that the impediment was Hawthorne's Puritan conscience, "which would not let him unrestrainedly enjoy a rose unless he could feel convinced that both the rose and he deserved it" (II, 143).

objects. They are poor aesthetics, but good morality. Hawthorne's interest in art objects is the same as his attention to all things—he reads them for what they represent, as if (to paraphrase Julian) they were people. The simplest kind of moral reading is the emblematic, and *The Marble Faun* contains a score of emblems like the statue of Innocence on the first page, or the Laocoön, or the stained-glass windows which Kenyon reads for us as "a most forcible emblem of the different aspect of religious truth" (Chap. xxxiii, p. 351). Subtler readings are necessary for other emblems, such as the sketches of husband-murder made by Miriam, or Kenyon's bust of Donatello, which variously serves to picture Donatello's moral state, Kenyon's attitude towards his subject and himself, and the entire process of artistic creation.

A handful of the more famous works are emblems not to Hawthorne but to his characters, who reveal their natures by their comments. For example, Miriam's response to Kenyon's statue of Cleopatra displays the natures of the two people and their relationship, just as the opening chapters of the novel, placed in the sculpture hall of the Vatican, set forth each of the main characters in the light of his attitude to art in general and to the Marble Faun in particular. Of special interest is the use of the portrait of Beatrice Cenci and of the statue of Pope Julius. The painting evokes the story of Beatrice Cenci, well known to the nineteenth century, and through it the whole force of the relationship between Miriam and Hilda and their involvement in guilt and innocence. The statue of Pope Julius is unusual in that it is the only art object about which three characters agree—Kenyon the man of marble, Miriam the lady of the sorrows, and Donatello the child of nature are united under his Christian blessing in one of the most complex chapters of the book. The clue to why Hawthorne used this technique so extensively lies in the *Italian Notebooks*. Speaking of the varied responses we make to a painting, he says, "Each man interprets the hieroglyphic in his own way; and the painter, perhaps, had a meaning which none of them have reached; or possibly he put forth a riddle without himself knowing the solution." A picture may be "a great symbol, proceeding out of a great mind; but if it means one thing, it seems to mean a thousand, and, often, opposite things" (pp. 331–332). With this attitude in mind, it was possible for Hawthorne to characterize his people through their responses to art, and by following these responses it is possible for us to comprehend that characterization.

The use of art as a thematic element built into the structure of

Hawthorne's thought has been explored by other critics. Millicent Bell concludes concerning *The Marble Faun* that "the theme of art is Hawthorne's major one." Roy R. Male points out that "the parallel between sculpture and life is introduced in the title, established in the first paragraph, and maintained throughout the book. The process of transfiguration is as central in art as it is in life." [7] The exact nature of Hawthorne's attitude to art in *The Marble Faun* is as difficult to determine as his ethical concepts, but the point important to our present purpose is that concepts of art and concepts of morality are so closely wedded to each other that it is not possible to discuss one without the other. In other words, none of these scenes could have taken place in a romance set in America because they rely for their meaning on art objects which exist only in Italy.

I

Hawthorne's use of art for characterization would be very strained, of course, if his characters were not artists of a sort, who define their natures by their attitudes towards their occupation. Those critics who see Kenyon as Hawthorne's spokesman throughout (as he is occasionally) will find difficulty in explaining why the novelist consistently reveals the limitations of both his sententiousness and his skill. Kenyon's nature must be understood, in fact, through the misinterpretations of Donatello's and Miriam's remarks about art which his affection for Hilda leads him to make. Again, Miriam's motives in occupying herself with art—escape and self-obsession—are as indicative as is Donatello's inability to respond to art at all. And Hilda? First in her response to the portrait of Beatrice Cenci and then consistently with other works, she shows the duality typical of her reactions to the world. Her first response stems from a great intuitive sympathy; her second from a cold, harsh, acquired dogmatism. Since her attitude to art both reveals her nature and dominates her reactions to people, the more carefully one studies her artistic behavior, the less simple, the less unreal, and the less ideal she becomes. Just how admirable, for instance, is her total dedication to looking at pictures? Given as much delicacy and sensitivity as she possesses, nonetheless does not the use to which she puts her fine qualities mark her as deeply flawed by narrow-mindedness? Though Hawthorne admired artists,

---

[7] Bell, *Hawthorne's View of the Artist* (New York, 1962), p. 91; Male, *Hawthorne's Tragic Vision* (Austin, Texas, 1957), p. 164.

he was under no illusions about them or their calling. "A genuine love of painting and sculpture," he wrote in the *Notebooks*, "and perhaps of music, seems often to have distinguished men capable of every social crime, and to have formed a fine and hard enamel over their characters. Perhaps it is because such tastes are artificial, the product of cultivation, and, when highly developed, imply a great remove from natural simplicity" (p. 317). It seems to me that these words contain the key to the characterization of not just Miriam and Kenyon, but of Hilda too.

It is in this Roman colony of artists that Hawthorne finds his people who have a "propriety of their own." In both his journal and *The Marble Faun* he is sure that he found qualities among artists not present among other groups. Of the people assembled for the chapter entitled "An Aesthetic Company" he says,

> They were not wholly confined within the sordid compass of practical life; they had a pursuit which, if followed faithfully out, would lead them to the beautiful, and always had a tendency thitherward. . . . Their actual business (though they talked about it very much as other men talk of cotton, politics, flour-barrels, and sugar) necessarily illuminated their conversation with something akin to the ideal. . . . The atmosphere ceased to be precisely that of common life; a faint, mellow tinge, such as we see in pictures, mingled itself with the lamplight. (Chap. xv, p. 164)

Why not, then, set the story amongst artists in New England? Because, as Kenyon tells us, "Rome is not like one of our New England villages, where we need the permission of each individual neighbor for every act that we do, every word that we utter, and every friend that we make or keep. In these particulars the papal despotism allows us freer breath than our native air" (Chap. xii, p. 133).

It is essential that the characters in *The Marble Faun* have complete freedom of movement, and this is given to them by residence in the artists' colony of Rome. It is one of the few situations that will work on the level of everyday reality to explain not just the intimacy but the very presence of characters as diverse as these, especially if one of the major themes of the novel is (as I believe) the conflict of Old and New Worlds. Hilda and Kenyon fit easily into their environment, even on the most drably naturalistic levels. Their intimacy with Donatello, representative of an ancient, noble, and rural Italian family, is easily explained:

His boyish passion for Miriam has introduced him familiarly to
our little circle; and our republican and artistic simplicity of intercourse has included this young Italian, on the same terms as one of
ourselves. But, if we paid due respect to rank and title, we should
bend reverentially to Donatello, and salute him as his Exellency the
Count di Monte Beni. (Chap. xii, p. 127)

The more mysterious and socially equally remote Miriam can also
join the group: "There was an ambiguity about this young lady,
which, though it did not necessarily imply anything wrong, would
have operated unfavorably as regarded her reception in society,
anywhere but in Rome" (Chap. iii, p. 35). Or again, "Nowhere
else but in Rome, and as an artist, could she hold a place in society
without giving some clew to her past life" (Chap. xii, p. 133).

If Miriam's freedom to join the artistic world sets the story off
on its course, then it is her freedom to leave it again that controls
all the later events. She can wander at will through Tuscany in
search of reunion with Donatello. Her disappearance, however, is
the direct cause of Hilda's visit to the Palazzo Cenci and consequent confinement. Apparently, again, it is Miriam and Donatello's
return to Rome and willing surrender of their own freedom of
action that release Hilda. Previous to her contact with Miriam's
guilt, Hilda was "an example of the freedom of life which it is
possible for a female artist to enjoy at Rome. . . . The customs of
artist life bestow such liberty upon the sex, which is elsewhere re-
stricted within so much narrower limits" (Chap. vi, p. 71). From
this point of view *The Marble Faun* begins to look like Hawthorne's
attempt to define the limits of moral responsibility or (if one prefers) of free will. All four characters make choices concerning their
actions and obligations, one action necessitating another, creating
a chain between the four which can be broken by one bad choice—
and all those choices are made in an atmosphere where freedom is
highest, where the ideal is closest, where pressure from incidental
personages or from society is at its lowest.

In this free environment (which could not have existed in
America), the causes behind each choice are quite clear and seem
to be both conscious and unconscious. Conscious are such acts as
Miriam's early refusals to have her husband murdered, Hilda's de-
livery of the package, and Donatello's surrender. Unconscious are
Kenyon's inability to respond to Miriam's need, Miriam's assent
to the murder, and Donatello's varied feelings towards Miriam.
Each of the characters has different views about the amount of free

choice he is exercising, usually with Miriam seeing none and Hilda claiming all. In Hawthorne's view, most of the choices show a mixture of conscious and unconscious, as is most clearly seen in Hilda's rejection of Miriam after the murder. Where his characters choose between free will and determinism, Hawthorne, typically, will have both. His cautious attitude is expressed in the question posed several times concerning a half-completed sculpture: has the face been in the block of marble since the beginning, merely waiting for its time to come, or is the sculptor's creation of that particular image absolutely free? He gives no answer, but it is perhaps significant that another major motif of the novel is the "ramble," the apparently objectiveless, unplanned wandering which leads to a climactic and seemingly predestined event.

There are many more uses to which Hawthorne put the artistic environment surrounding him. They flicker through the texture of the novel, but it is almost impossible, and certainly unnecessary, to pin them down. As Henry James wrote, *The Marble Faun* contains "a great many light threads of symbolism, which shimmer in the texture of the tale, but which are apt to break and remain in our fingers if we attempt to handle them." [8] Such threads are the picturing of the three artists' studios, the identification of sculpture as masculine and painting as feminine, the relationship between creations of God and man, and the constant setting of big scenes amidst the pallid glimmer of statuary or the gloss of marbled rooms. James went on to say that such threads "belong more to the surface of his work than to its stronger interest." Hawthorne did not agree. Anticipating James's metaphor, he asked in the last chapter that the readers of his tale "accept it at its worth, without tearing its web apart, with the idle purpose of discovering how the threads have been knit together." Already we have sufficiently disobeyed him.

Rome offered Hawthorne much more than a colony of artists. He must have been struck by the number of things Italian that, with no change at all in their mundane nature, could simply assume a fairyland atmosphere. We can see him playing with the thought when he uses his most Gothic manner to introduce the Spectre of the Catacombs, and at once undercuts the Gothic by saying that "the spectre might have made a considerable impression on the sculptor's nerves, only that he was in the habit of observing similar figures, almost every day, reclining on the Spanish steps, and wait-

---

[8] *Hawthorne,* p. 169.

ing for some artist to invite them within the magic realm of picture" (Chap. IV, p. 45). The Spectre is the most lurid and improbable of all his characters, but, says Hawthorne, "It may occur to the reader, that there was really no demand for so much rumor and speculation in regard to an incident, which might well enough have been explained without going many steps beyond the limits of probability" (Chap. IV, p. 51). Perhaps, he suggests, the Spectre is a beggar, a criminal, or a harmless lunatic. Certainly "his pertinacity need not seem so very singular to those who consider how slight a link serves to connect these vagabonds of idle Italy with any person that may . . . betray the slightest interest in their fortunes." His own pertinacity in offering these explanations shows how important it was to him to have his cake and eat it, to keep the mundane and the mysterious, and how valuable Italy was in providing him with what he wanted.

Many of the improbabilities of the plot of *The Marble Faun* can be explained by referring them to the very real social and political conditions of mid-nineteenth century Italy, occupied by the French, divided into rival states, and united by the subterranean operations of a politically active Vatican. Admittedly, Hawthorne may not have taken pains over working out the narrative. Indeed Mrs. Hawthorne wrote, "I am surprised to find that Mr. Hawthorne was so absorbed in Italy that he had no idea that the story, as such, was interesting!" [9] In the original version, much was left (perhaps deliberately) unclear, but the conclusion added to the second edition explains events on a level that is as certainly plausible as it is certainly romantic, attributing them to the tenebrous operations of civic and religious powers under the necessity of treading lightly amongst the affairs of both aristocrats and foreign citizens. One does not wish to exaggerate the credibility of the events in *The Marble Faun*, but one must note that—so successfully has Hawthorne established his fairyland atmosphere—the lack of "magic" in its events makes the tale less reliant on the supernatural than any of his preceding works. *The Marble Faun* has no Faustian seer of the psyche, no long-lost deed or inherited curse, no satanic mesmerist or Veiled Lady. Such wondrous agencies give way in *The Marble Faun* to the structure of Italian society. Hilda is arrested because of her connection with a crime of violence; the police cannot help Kenyon find her because other authorities are handling her case; she reappears as the result of Miriam's ability to strike bargains and "pull strings."

---

9 Julian Hawthorne, II, 247.

II

On the level of theme as well as plot, the Italian background is essential, for one of the themes handled at length is a conflict which involves, on the one hand, America, Protestantism, youth, innocence, and pragmatism, and, on the other hand, Italy, Catholicism, age, sin, and aestheticism. The conflict is most obvious in aesthetic matters. Hilda's delicate but original talent gives way, she becomes a copyist, and her devotion to the "mighty old masters" is a form of "slavery." Hawthorne does not approve the decay of originality, though in Hilda's case it is replaced by her much greater ability as a copyist. Certainly, however, Hilda's slavery to the old masters must be replaced by a more critical, safer attitude. The sense that Hawthorne is conveying seems to be that, while one can learn a great deal from the old masters, they can also destroy the person who is both sensitive and unwitting. The same thought is explicit concerning the effect of Italy as a whole. What Hilda realizes when she talks with Miriam after the murder is that "the sins of generations past have created an atmosphere of sin for those that follow" (Chap. xxiii, p. 247). The idea is further developed in Kenyon's advice to Donatello:

> You should go with me to my native country. . . . In that fortunate land, each generation has only its own sins and sorrows to bear. Here, it seems as if all the weary and dreary Past were piled upon the back of the Present. (Chap. xxxiii, p. 347)

The conflict appears most strongly in the clash of religions, which is not so much between two systems (Catholic and Protestant) as between two attitudes towards salvation (penance and good works). Paralleling the previously mentioned division between the conscious and the unconscious in the debate over the boundaries of free choice, here we have a metaphysical framework created by Hawthorne within which the individual characters take their own changing postures. Donatello, beginning as a pagan, collapses into a penitential despair which is concretely displayed—and admonished—in the chapter entitled "Scenes by the Way." Donatello is to find the path to salvation not through a "superstitious" penance, efficacious as that may be psychologically, but through joining Miriam, who had also despaired of the future, in a more practical expiation. In the climactic chapter "The Bronze Pontiff's Benediction," the Protestant sculptor Kenyon, speaking as the agent of the Catholic Pope Julius, urges them to effort and sacrifice. Their "sombre and thoughtful happiness" will come out of "toil, sacrifice, prayer, penitence, and earnest effort to right things" (Chap. xxxv, p. 370), a blending of the Catholic and Protestant attitudes. The most notable of their efforts towards right things is their submission to earthly justice. But neither Kenyon nor Hawthorne rejects entirely the forms of penance. The story of Hilda's sufferings seems specifically designed to illustrate their psychological (but not their metaphysical) efficacy, for in her extremity, and though she is a heretic, the form of confession is her salvation. Neatly she distinguishes between the acceptable and the unacceptable; Providence, "the direct impulse of Heaven," leads her to confession, but "God forbid that I should ask absolution from mortal man!" Perhaps Hawthorne would have made a happy Episcopalian.

It is not to my purpose to investigate further the nature of Hawthorne's religious beliefs in *The Marble Faun*, but to point out that the doctrines involved here contain all of the themes which occupied him in earlier works, and that their exploration by means of the confrontation between a son and daughter of the Puritans and the representatives of Catholic Italy creates a complexity and concreteness of situation he had not previously achieved. Perhaps no church but St. Peter's, no city but Rome, no country but Italy, could have provided such an opportunity, and this is the reason why his descriptions of church, city, and country revolve around the very visible symbols of faith, suffering, and salvation.

Eventually, however, the religious conflict becomes mingled with all the other themes apparent in *The Marble Faun* and all join under some greater heading, to which it is properly difficult to give a name. We have increasingly come to understand that Hawthorne is more wise than didactic, that his books do not carry messages, that he raises issues and presents alternative solutions, but offers few judgments. His tale is of what has been rather than of what should be. There cannot, surely, be another article arguing that Hawthorne was either for or against the fortunate fall.[10] *The Marble Faun* contains many mighty themes, no one of which stands as *the* theme of the romance as a whole. The background material

---

[10] I succumb to temptation myself, however, in order to suggest that the purpose of the debates between Kenyon and Hilda and Miriam on the subject of the fortunate fall is not to give Hawthorne's viewpoint at all, but to show the change in Kenyon himself. That he would be tempted to agree with Miriam shows how close he has moved towards accepting the European viewpoint; that he would immediately retreat from this position at Hilda's whim shows the nature of the compromise he makes in order to preserve what he can of his expensive new happiness.

suggests that one way of thinking of the book that will give each theme no more than its proper importance is that the book is a meditation on the subject of time.

III

There are three aspects of time which especially concern Hawthorne: the past, the present, and the eternal. These three abstractions relate differently to each other according to which lesser theme is under consideration. Occasionally they appear to conflict, but more often they interlock: past and present, placed together, produce the eternal. In the general opposition between the present and the past, we have on the side of the present America, Puritanism, the conscious choice, the person as individual, the psychological particularity, and the freely willed act. On the side of the past are Italy, Catholicism and paganism, the unconscious passion, the person as representative of his forefathers, the metaphysical generalization, and the predetermined act. The movement of the romance as a whole is to suggest that this apparent opposition is unreal and that its resolution lies in the sense of the eternal.

Let us see this pattern first in the characters. Donatello is a creature from the pagan or pre-religious past, a time of moral ignorance. His type has recurred since antiquity through the generations of his forefathers, but in the present it is anomalous and doomed to extinction. Psychologically, he has no sense of past or future and lives only for the present moment. His kinship is with the ephemeral animals (not with enduring art), his wine loses its savor if it is not drunk at once, and his most characteristic expression is the evanescence of the dance. Through his crime he at once develops a sense of the past, joining Miriam in the "innumerable confraternity of guilty ones," becoming one of "the majestic and guilty shadows, that, from ages long gone by, have haunted the blood-stained city" (Chap. xix, p. 207). His new sense of the unalterability of his individual past, now graven into eternity, destroys his belief in the future and the present, and he collapses into despair. But his reunion with Miriam awakens him to the impersonal, metaphysical eternal: the possibility of salvation.

Miriam enters the story obsessed by the past and plunged into despair. She is connected with all the old religions—Etruscan, Roman, Jewish, and Catholic—but she herself cannot find God. The subjects of her paintings are Biblical and bloody, the constant repetition through history of the same emotions, and those sketches of the present which she executes are "dreams," marred always by the watching figure of the past. She achieves a temporary release into the present through dancing with Donatello, a purpose for the future through the love springing from the crime, and a hope for salvation (and hence escape from the past) through their reunion. The strongest link between these two people is the Spectre of the Catacombs, the man crushed and enslaved by the past, despairing of salvation, unconscious of the present. To Miriam he represents all the chains of the past; as soon as he is dead, she is free from the worst. He is also the Satyr to Donatello's Faun. The two have come down through history together, and Donatello destroys the Spectre's primeval gloom only at the price of his own Arcadia. The theme is not new to Hawthorne, but it is much broader than ever before and it is laboring the issue to point out that such characters could not exist were they not made possible by the ancientness of their backgrounds and country.

Contrasted to all this European oppressiveness are the representatives of the New World, Hilda and Kenyon. Hawthorne, it seems, recognized the utterly conventional distinctions between the creatures of the Old and the New Worlds, but he was not so greatly confident of their magnitude as most of his contemporaries. Before knowledge of the crime, Hilda can wander intact, unaware, through all the nastiness of history and humanity that contaminates Rome. Psychologically, she is aware only of her Puritan past and the idealization of the greater past in painting. Through her painting of the old masters, however, her remoteness is threatened, and then the crime, her perception of Miriam's guilt, her confession, her confinement by the spiritual-political authorities, bring her into increasingly close touch with a much more extensive and burdensome past. Hawthorne expresses the growth in this relationship by her responses to paintings, which show her less and less able to continue her idealization, more and more involved in the emotions of the present, and finally able to work out an acceptable (if not admirable) adjustment between the two. Kenyon's development is similar. The "man of marble," the man who controls his strong perceptions of both history and the present by eternizing them in marble (see, for example, the description of the statue of Cleopatra), loses the safety of detachment through Hilda. With her disappearance he abandons his work and is unmoved even by the discovery of a new statue. Previously he was able to control time by detaching himself from it, but now the acts of the proponents of the past bring him very much into the concerns of the immediate present, an event which is well symbolized in the Carnival scene.[11]

The relationship between the characters and time is capable of much more complex interpretation, but the point to note here is that the interlocking of past and present to create the eternal is inherent in the world which Hawthorne chooses as his setting— not just the artistic world, with its eternizing processes, but the world of Rome, the Eternal City. Throughout all his romances, one is conscious that the events Hawthorne describes are always struggling out of the confines of the time in which they are happening into a plane where they are the re-enactment of an eternally recurring event. The struggle is more successful in *The Marble Faun* than in the American romances because in Italy every object that Hawthorne touches lights up with historical connotations which are integral to his purposes. (To see how pervasively this is true, one might look at some very ordinary passages, such as the descriptions of the fountain in Chapter v, of the market-place of Perugia in Chapter xxxiv, and of the palace in which Hilda lives in Chapter xLiv.)

The geography and history of Rome are exploited on page after page. One of the most extended passages is the "moonlight ramble" leading to the murder (Chaps. xvi-xviii), where Hawthorne takes us on what was and is, literally, a Cook's Tour of Rome. On one side of the picture is the lighthearted group of artists, rambling among familiar sights and cheerfully singing "Hail, Columbia!" Hawthorne accentuates the conventionality of their tour, the normality of their responses, the jollity of their behavior. But accompanying them is the spectral model, moving on his useless penitential mission, gradually increasing the anguish of Miriam and Donatello until his death results—so that we have on the other side all the gloom of sin, guilt, punishment, murder, and blood. Occupying the common ground are the sights of the Eternal City: the Fountain of the Trevi, Trajan's Forum, the Coliseum, the Arch of Constantine, the Forum, the Campidoglio, and finally the Tarpeian Rock. Each of these famous sights is read by one or more of the characters for its moral significance. As Hilda says, "There are sermons in stones . . . and especially in the stones of Rome."

---

[11] The motif of the Carnival scene is well expressed in a remark made by Christof Wegelin in another connection: "Thus, the closeness of the past [in Rome] strongly suggests the transitoriness of earthly things, and according to their temperament people find either sorrow or comfort in the thought" ("Europe in Hawthorne's Fiction," *ELH*, XIV, 223, Sept., 1947).

The Trevi raises the opposition between art and nature, between Italian aestheticism and American practicality. The column in Trajan's Forum, "a great, solid fact of the Past," stirs Miriam and Hilda into another of their disagreements over the value of art and humanity and places the argument in the context of the eternal. The Coliseum contrasts the light and the dark in the strongest terms—Roman altars and Christian shrines, the damned spectators and the saved martyrs. It is a place of "crime and suffering" which has gained "a more than common sanctity." Girls romp amongst the penitents. While Miriam writhes unseen in anguish, Hilda comments, "How delightful this is!" The Arch of Titus causes Hawthorne to remark, "The very ghosts of that massive and stately epoch have so much density that the actual people of today seem the thinner of the two." In the Forum, the gulf of Curtius evokes the conflict between Miriam and Hilda over the destiny of man, the inevitability of defeat claimed by Miriam, and the salvation through virtue by Hilda. The statue of Marcus Aurelius repeats the debate in different terms. And finally the Tarpeian Rock, which provides Hilda with "a beautiful view of the city," enables Miriam to call forth the spirits of all the guilty souls by whose destruction "innocent souls were saved." All this before the plot moves an inch.

Such chapters are so dense with material that critical analysis is wordy and impertinent. Their density is typical of several other passages of the book, notably the other two lengthy rambles: by Kenyon and Donatello through Tuscany, and by Hilda through the galleries and churches of Rome. Each ramble ends in a climactic event: murder, marriage, confession. If one reads them for the story, regarding them as so much atmosphere, then they must seem the most tedious, pedantic, and amateurish of emotional impediments. If *The Marble Faun* were a Gothic romance, the judgment would be valid, for the Gothic writers wrote for a single reading; that over, they have little else to offer. Hawthorne, however, wrote for the second, third, and fourth reading. It is only when we have lost our surprise at the plot that we start seeing the meaning. A clear plot would give us a clear moral, or, to put the idea from Hawthorne's point of view, an unclear plot makes an obscure moral. If it is true that Hawthorne wanted to avoid a clear moral, then he reflected the meditational nature of his thinking by using the "ramble" to organize the development of his narrative. Each ramble reflects his ideas about the operation of the conscious and unconscious (or free will and determinism)—people wander, apparently at their will and certainly without foresight, but their casual journey ends up in a place that seems then to be the one possible terminus. Each ramble also places the events in their proper perspective as part of the marble of time, makes us see them as universal and eternal rather than romantic and unique, extends them backwards through the course of history (Christian, classical, pagan) so that they are repeated in an unbroken chain back to Arcadia and forward to—what? As F. O. Matthiessen wrote, "Thus perpetually for Hawthorne the shimmer of the now was merely the surface of the deep pool of history." [12]

Hawthorne himself said of *The Marble Faun*, "But, in fact, if I have written anything well, it should be this Romance; for I have never thought or felt more deeply, or taken more pains." [13] If we have preferred *The Scarlet Letter*, it is because we have judged the two novels by the same standards, when in fact *The Marble Faun* is as new to the American fiction of 1860 as *The Scarlet Letter* was to that of 1850. It shares with *The Scarlet Letter* the refusal to make simplistic moral judgments about the ways of God and man, which Hawthorne believes in the end to be inscrutable. But the ethical centre of *The Marble Faun* is quite different from that of *The Scarlet Letter*, and so is its technique. The meaning of the novel cannot be grasped by extracting tags or by elaborating plot summaries to prove a particular point of view, because Hawthorne's primary interest is the moral organization of the universe as it is seen by different types of men. The novel consists of a series of shifting perspectives in space and time, and we find out what men are by what they think about material things. We are in fact much nearer to the universe of James, Proust, and Joyce than to that of Melville or Mark Twain. The novel deserves comparison not with *The Scarlet Letter* but with those other products of the impact of Italy on the mid-Victorian mind, *Romola* (1863) and *The Ring and the Book* (1868–69). *The Marble Faun* is twice as long as any of Hawthorne's other works, largely because it contains many times the number of concrete details. Rather than analyze the larger elements of the novel, I have concentrated on suggesting in this essay that it is only through immersion in those details that we can enter into the world of *The Marble Faun* and so approach the problems of theme, characterization, and meaning. The superiority of *The Marble Faun* lies in its "backdrops of scenery," meticulously described, and lifted from a land which offered opportunities not available in his homeland for Hawthorne to exercise his imagination. Instead of laboriously creating his Faery Land, at last he found it waiting for him.

---

[12] *American Renaissance,* p. 355.
[13] Julian Hawthorne, II, 99–100.

[Mask and Dance Motifs in *The Marble Faun*]

. . . As in *The Blithedale Romance*, the key role played by mask-ing and the dance in *The Marble Faun* derives from Hawthorne's own observations expanded and intensified by his long interest in these traditional pageant-symbols. The subtitle, "The Romance of Monte Beni," may remind us that the ancestral estate of Donatello is identified with Arcadia. "Come in wild Faun," says Miriam, "and tell me the latest news from Arcady!" [1] Donatello is fre-quently described as gamboling and dancing; and Miriam, painting a rustic dance, chooses him as model for the "wildest dancer of them all." [2] But by now we know that in Hawthorne's work crisis and catastrophe invariably follow dancing and merriment. In Chapter X, entitled "The Sylvan Dance," Hawthorne thus fore-shadows trouble for his two revelers:

> Donatello snapped his fingers above his head, as fauns and satyrs taught us first to do, and seemed to radiate jollity out of his whole nimble person. Nevertheless, there was a kind of dim apprehension in his face, as if he dreaded that a moment's pause might break the spell, and snatch away the sportive companion whom he had waited for through so many dreary months.
>
> "Dance, dance!" cried he, joyously. "If we take breath, we shall be as we were yesterday. There, now, is the music, just beyond this clump of trees. Dance, Miriam, dance!" [3]

A little further on the author compares the merry crew led by the Faun to the gay figures carved on an antique vase or an an-cient sarcophagus, and characteristically points out that once you

---

From "Ritual and Reality: Mask and Dance Motifs in Hawthorne's Fiction," *Philological Quarterly*, XXXIV (January, 1955), 66–70. By permission of the Department of Publications of The University of Iowa and the author. [Textual citations are to the Riverside Edition of Hawthorne's works, edited by George Parsons Lathrop.]
[1] Frank Davidson in "Toward a Re-evaluation of *The Blithedale Romance*," *NEQ*, XXV (1952), 374–383, even asserts that the main theme of this novel is the tragedy attendant on ambiguities which man believes to be real but which are by nature veiled.
[2] *Works*, VI, 55.
[3] *Works*, VI, 64.

have seen the fallen youth, overturned chariot, fainting maiden or other "tragic incident" which is always portrayed, "you can look no more at the festal portions of the scene, except with reference to this one slightly suggested doom and sorrow." [4] Here in condensed form is Hawthorne's attitude toward the dance and toward all revelry which is either over-exuberant or coldly formal and lacking in spontaneity. This attitude is also reflected in the dour note—almost the tone of a kill-joy—which he sounds in his *Note-Book* descriptions of the Roman Carnival. This bit of damnation with faint praise is typical: "I can conceive of its being rather agreeable than otherwise, up to the age of twenty." [5] When he saw the Carnival the next year (1859), he was somewhat more impressed.[6] But afterwards in England he wrote crankily, "Upon my honor, I never in my life knew a shallower joke than the Carnival at Rome." [7] Nonetheless he admitted that it fascinated him and he not only described it at some length in his notes but elaborated these a good deal in *The Marble Faun*. Later he blamed the length of the work on the fact that he could not bring himself to cut or cancel his many descriptions of Roman and Florentine scenes, which he had so enjoyed penning.[8] Among these scenes we may reckon those of the Carnival.

As in *Blithedale* he adopted some factual details *in toto*, changed others slightly, and transfused still others almost beyond recognition in accordance with his purpose. Kenyon, like Hawthorne, is assaulted with unusual vigor by the throwers of confetti and vegetables. Kenyon notices the shallowness and pretense of most of the gaiety, as had Hawthorne himself. Various types of masks are described in approximately parallel phrases in the notes and the novel. Among other details Hawthorne records the use of white dominoes, and in one of the most telling bits of symbolism in *The Marble Faun* he pictures the joyful Hilda, purged of her emphatic guilt, in a white domino—a stark contrast to the black masks of the penitent murderers, Miriam and Donatello.[9] Donatello is also shown earlier as wearing a mask which is "featureless," and his aspect is "ghastly and startling." When confronted by Kenyon

---

[4] *Works*, VI, 107.
[5] *Works*, VI, 110. Cited also by Dorothy Waples in "Suggestions for Interpreting *The Marble Faun*," *AL*, XIII (1941), 237.
[6] "Passages from the French and Italian Notebooks," in *Works*, X, 80. See also pp. 68–69.
[7] *Works*, X, 486–491.
[8] Julian Hawthorne, *Nathaniel Hawthorne and His Wife*, II, 181.
[9] Caroline Ticknor, *Hawthorne and His Publisher* (Boston, 1913), p. 219.

he returns stare for stare with his "hollow eyes" and hurries away without speaking.[10] In penance for his crime he has abrogated his individuality; he has become a worm of the dust.[11] Hawthorne amplifies this theme of mortal insignificance by working into the pageant of maskers a parade of the dignitaries of Rome. In the notes his eye is on the Grand Duke; in the novel he stresses the falsity and pretentiousness of these grandees, who behind their gaudy finery are "illusive shadows, every one." [12]

By means of pageant and dance, then, Hawthorne partially fused his romance of sin, growth and atonement with its cluttered Italian background. In the final celebration Miriam and Donatello are whirled along in a saturnalia of penitence. Concerning this episode some interesting commentary was exchanged by Hawthorne and his friend, the historian John Lothrop Motley. From Motley's balcony Hawthorne had viewed part of the Carnival on his first visit to Rome. Later Motley wrote to him, in a letter dated March 29, 1860: "The way in which the two victims dance through the Carnival on the last day is very striking. It is like a Greek tragedy in its effect, without being in the least Greek." [13] To this Hawthorne replied from Bath, England (April 1, 1860):

> You are certainly that Gentle Reader for whom all my books were exclusively written. Nobody else ... has ever said exactly what I love to hear. It is most satisfactory to be hit upon the raw, to be shot straight through the heart. ... You take the book precisely as I meant it; and if your note had come a few days sooner, I believe I would have printed it in a postscript which I have added to the second edition, because it explains better than I found possible to do the way in which my romance ought to be taken.[14]

How ought it to be taken? In it one may detect the Greek view of an inexorable fate against which men struggle in vain, but more central is the Christian theme of sin, penitence, and atonement through suffering. However, the tragedy of Miriam and Donatello is ceremonialized by their participation in the wild Bacchic dance

---

[10] *Works,* VI, 501, 505–506, 510.
[11] *Works,* 446–447.
[12] For additional comment and criticism see Newton Arvin, *Hawthorne* (Boston, 1929), pp. 258–263.
[13] *Works,* VI, 500.
[14] Reprinted in "Biographical Sketch of Nathaniel Hawthorne," by George Parsons Lathrop, *Works,* XII, 537.

of the Carnival. The forward action of the book has practically ceased before the festivities begin, and the pattern of their penitence and fate is unfolded in a dramatic ritual highly analogous to the tragedies of Aeschylus in particular.[15] In these scenes Hilda, Kenyon and other spectators function somewhat as did the old choral commentators. On the other hand the lushness of detail suggests paganism in decadence, Roman opulence rather than Attic simplicity.

Historically, then, the mask and dance as motifs appealed to Hawthorne because, in the Puritan tradition with which he was so familiar, they stood for collective evil, particularly devil-worship, pagan sensuality, and lack of restraint. In "Young Goodman Brown" and "The Maypole of Merry Mount" the dance is a mental and moral debauch, a wild abandonment of self to Satan on the part of the dancers. In "A Select Party," *The House of the Seven Gables*, and *The Blithedale Romance* the dance seems at first the opposite—a strained and unnatural pose rather than a dionysiac whirl. In all cases, however, the object of the dancers is to shut out reality. In *The Marble Faun* the dance is both an escape and a penitential rite.

Aesthetically, masking and the dance appealed to Hawthorne because such relatively stiff and formal pageantry furnished the perfect means of objectifying and dramatizing—as in a morality play—one of his favorite themes, irresponsible illusion shattered by the harsh but solid realities of duty and the need for responsibility.

---

[15] Paul Elmer More has compared *The House of the Seven Gables* to the tragedies of Aeschylus in *Shelburne Essays, First Series* (New York, 1904), pp. 39–40.

Charles R. Smith, Jr.

The Structural Principle of
The Marble Faun

Very little of the critical attention paid to Hawthorne's *The Marble Faun* has centered on its structure. This paper will examine the basic structural principle of the novel—the plan behind the order in which the events of the plot occur. Most of the critics have been concerned primarily with the novel's theme, with the structure receiving only brief and uncomplimentary notice. Few of the later critics have differed very much with the unfavorable judgement in Henry James' *Hawthorne:*

> The art of narration in [*The Marble Faun*] seems to me more at fault than in the author's other novels. The story straggles and wanders, is dropped and taken up again, and towards the close lapses into an almost fatal vagueness.[1]

The only article devoted exclusively to structural analysis is Merle E. Brown's "The Structure of *The Marble Faun.*" Brown believes the book to be constructed around "a single idea, the transformation from innocence to experience, repeated, with no major deviations, four times." [2] He traces this transformation in each of the major characters: Miriam's immediately after the murder of the model, Donatello's after a long period of soul searching, Hilda's after unburdening herself in the confessional, and Kenyon's only after the disappearance of Hilda in the final chapters.

Although Brown is fairer to the novel than the other critics, his analysis still leaves a great deal unexplained. It does not satisfactorily account for the arrangement of the chapters before the murder scene, a part of the book under particularly heavy critical attack.[3] Nor does it account for the order in which the changes take place. Finally, there are quite major deviations in the kinds of transformations and in the characters, both before and after.

Reprinted from *Thoth,* III (Winter, 1962), 32–38, with the permission of the Department of English, Syracuse University.
[1] Great Seal Books (Ithaca, 1956), p. 134.
[2] *American Literature,* XXVIII (1956–7), 303.
[3] In this regard, see especially Rudolph Von Abele, *The Death of the Artist* (The Hague, 1955), pp. 95 ff.

Brown's interpretation seems somewhat oversimplified. The transformations do take place, and in the order he traces, but they seem not the structural principle in themselves but a part of a more complex structure. This oversimplification may result from a misreading of the novel's central theme. Brown states it as "the simple fact that sin is a condition of all human life, that we are all sinners whether we like to admit the fact or not." [4] It is true that Hawthorne was aware of the constant presence of sin in humankind, but this is not all that he was saying in the novel. Probably the clearest explanation of the central theme can be found in Donald A. Ringe's "Hawthorne's Psychology of the Head and Heart." Ringe sees the theme as Hawthorne's attempt to present the two alternative courses of action for man living in a world in which evil exists:

> In the Marble Faun, then, Hawthorne presents both of his solutions to the problem of life. Men can act in either of two ways in this evil world, and each way entails its own sacrifices and its own reward. If man is to develop the noblest qualities of mind and heart and so achieve true and profound insight into the problem of human existence, he must sin, incur the perilous state of isolation and sacrifice whatever happiness can be achieved in a troubled world. On the other hand, he may seek his earthly blisses and sacrifice his individuality in the common anonymity of ordinary life. [5]

Miriam and Donatello represent the first of these alternatives, Hilda and Kenyon the second. This understanding of the theme can lead to a more accurate understanding of the way the novel is constructed.

The action of *The Marble Faun* falls into seven major sections:
1. Initial characterization of Miriam, Hilda, Kenyon, and Donatello.
2. Explanation of the relationships between the characters.
3. Increase in the intensity of the Miriam-Donatello-model triangle, culminating in the murder scene, the novel's pivotal action.
4. Immediate after-effects of the murder: Miriam's transformation, Hilda's withdrawal, Donatello's exultation and despair.

At this point the story ceases to follow the characters as a group. The structure can be likened to the effect of a stone dropped into a

---

[4] p. 312.
[5] *PMLA,* LXV (1950), 132.

pool. The effects of the murder are shown first on those most immediately concerned, Miriam and Donatello, then on Hilda, the observer, and finally on Kenyon, the one farthest removed from it.
5. The full course of Donatello's transformation from faun to a human being of superior sensibility.
6. Hilda's gradual acceptance of the fact of evil, loss of artistic ability, and awakening to Kenyon's love.
7. Kenyon's loss of artistic ability and complete dedication to ordinary human emotion.

The final chapter brings all the characters together again in Rome, restating the theme in terms of the probable fate of each couple, and of the degree of insight which each is capable of attaining.

In the first section, Chapters I through VIII, the four main characters are introduced and fully described, so that the stage of intellectual and emotional development each has reached at the beginning of the action is made clear. Donatello's similarity to Praxiteles' statue of the faun is pointed out in the first chapter and further explored in the second. He remains throughout the first section as a happy, not quite human creature, worshipping Miriam as a dog might its mistress. His antipathy towards the model, for example, Hawthorne calls "not so much a human dislike or hatred, as one of those instinctive, unreasoning antipathies which the lower animals sometimes display" (p. 610).[6]

Miriam first appears to the reader as a dark and passionate beauty, shadowed by the sense of foreboding that pervades her fantastic explanation of the model. She is supplied with a vague but threatening past. Speaking of her paintings, Hawthorne demonstrates her rather melodramatically expressed feeling of isolation from society:

> There was one observable point, indeed, betokening that the artist relinquished, for her personal self, the happiness which she could so profoundly appreciate for others. In all these sketches of common life, and the affections that spiritualize it, a figure was portrayed apart. . . . Always it was the same figure, and always depicted with an expression of deep sadness; and in every instance, slightly as they were brought out, the face and form had the traits of Miriam's own. (p. 616)

Miriam's visit to Hilda's studio shows the contrasts between the

---

[6] All quotations are from *The Complete Novels and Selected Tales of Nathaniel Hawthorne,* ed. Norman H. Pearson (New York, 1937). The page numbers are cited in parentheses following the quotation.

two women. Hilda is also isolated: physically, in her tower dedi-
cated to virginity, and spiritually in her complete innocence, which
Miriam calls "a sharp steel sword" (p. 627). It is this militant innocence which lets her see in the portrait of Beatrice Cenci only
sorrow, while the experienced Miriam sees also a consciousness of
sin.

Of Kenyon we learn little in the first section, save that he is a
sculptor of some ability. A thoughtful man, he is the one among
them who seriously ponders the plight of Donatello, a faun in nineteenth-century Rome. The reader learns of his incipient love for
Hilda only through a brief reference in Chapter VII: "Kenyon the
sculptor . . . took note of [Hilda's] ethereal kiss, and wished that he
could have caught it in the air and got Hilda's leave to keep it"
(p. 629).

The second section, Chapters IX through XIV, concentrates on
the relationships which are developing between the major characters. The section follows the figure of Miriam as she wanders from
one to another, trying to find some understanding and consolation.
First she meets Donatello in the Borghese gardens.

Unable to convince Donatello that he should attempt to break off
his attachment for her, Miriam decides to enter his world for a
while. "Well, then, for this one hour, let me be such as he imagines
me. . . . He shall make me as natural as himself for this one hour"
(pp. 636–637). They revel in the "Sylvan Dance," which is described in the Arcadian imagery constantly associated with Donatello during the period before the murder. The model appears again,
breaking into Miriam's temporary escape from care and arousing
again Donatello's animal hatred. For the first time, Miriam comes
to fear the savagery which inspires him to say, "Shall I clutch him
by the throat? . . . Bid me do so and we are rid of him forever"
(p. 641). The link between the model and Miriam—some dark
crime with which they were both connected—is now revealed, and
Miriam predicts that only death will come of their meeting. As
they leave, the scene shifts to show Hilda and Kenyon in the role
they are to follow for most of the novel, observers of the relationship between Miriam and Donatello. Hilda can see no possibility
that Miriam will ever love Donatello; Kenyon can, but he despairs
of Hilda's ever loving him. As he tells Miriam when she visits his
studio, Hilda seems more than humanly perfect.

During the visit, Miriam attempts to unburden herself to Kenyon,
but finally keeps her silence, unable to believe that he has the sort
of sympathy that would really reach out to help her. Nor can she
turn to Hilda, because "Of sorrow, slender as she seems, Hilda

might bear a great burden; of sin, not a feather's weight" (p. 663). Feeling utterly alone, Miriam experiences "this perception of an infinite, shivering solitude, amid which we cannot come close enough to human beings to be warmed by them, and where they turn to cold, chilly shapes of mist" (p. 655).

Now that the situation is fully revealed, Hawthorne proceeds to the evening of the murder in the third section, Chapters XV through XVIII. Things begin quietly enough at an artist's party, but the face of the model turns up among some old drawings, and the model himself accosts Miriam as the group takes a sightseeing walk through the city. Again Donatello wants to kill him, but Miriam restrains him as she might have "a faithful hound" (p. 675). But when the model appears yet again in the Coliseum, Miriam's control slips and she goes almost mad for a moment. When Donatello stays with her even through this and her warnings, she resolves to unburden herself to him the next day. Relieved by her decision, she goes with the rest of the party to the Tarpeian Rock, lingering to answer Donatello's questions as the rest go on ahead.

> "Who are they . . . who have been flung over here in days gone by?" "Men that cumbered the world," she replied. "Men whose lives were the bane of their fellow creatures. . . ." "Was it well done? . . ." "It was well done." (pp. 687–688)

The model appears and approaches. Donatello springs at him, glances at Miriam, and throws him over the edge. Hawthorne has very carefully built the emotional tone between Miriam and Donatello, so that the murder seems believable but the responsibility almost impossible to fix. Miriam felt goaded beyond endurance; Donatello had been swayed by what she had just said, already hated the model, and perhaps was not human enough to know right from wrong. He sprang like an animal, saw permission in Miriam's eyes, and pushed. Miriam knew that she feared and hated the model, but did not know what had been in her eyes at the crucial moment. Who is culpable? Or is either?

The next section, Chapters XIX through XXIII, deals with the immediate effect of the murder on those concerned. Donatello was no longer the faun; now he was:

> the young man, whose form seemed to have dilated, and whose eyes blazed with the fierce energy that had suddenly inspired him. It had kindled him into a man; it had developed within him an intelligence which was no native characteristic of the Dona-

tello whom we have heretofore known. But that simple and joyous creature was gone forever. (p. 689)

Immediately after the murder, Donatello felt only a wild exultation, a joy that he and Miriam were now bound together by love and guilt. But by the next day, after seeing the model's body transfigured into that of a saintly monk, his new-found intelligence had made him despair of his soul because of his sin, and almost hate Miriam for her part in it.

Miriam had felt the same exultation, and she had accepted her love for Donatello and her responsibility for his act. No longer thinking only of herself, she is able to go against her own instincts and send him away, so that he might forget both her and his deed. Going to see Hilda, she discovers that Hilda had seen the murder, and seen in Miriam's eyes "a look of hatred, triumph, vengeance, and, as it were, joy at some unhoped-for relief" (p. 710). Hilda can offer neither sympathy nor relief, feeling that just her knowledge of the crime has destroyed the innocence of the world. Oppressed by her knowledge, Hilda feels she cannot seek help from Kenyon, for he wishes to love her. Kenyon's role in this section is quite small. Not directly connected to the murder, he has no part to play here.

The fifth section, Chapters XXIV through XXXV, shows the whole of Donatello's change from faun to man and his ascent from despair to a limited hope. Through Kenyon, the observer, the reader learns the family history and Donatello's original state. Donatello's loss of ability to communicate with the animals underscores his humanity, as his musings in the tower do his state of despair. He who was once so much a part of nature now cannot feel its beauty even as much as Kenyon. Through remorse and penitence, he gradually rises from his depth of isolation and despair. By the time he is united again with Miriam in Perugia, he has come to hope for at least forgiveness.

Chapters XXXVI through XLII shift back to Hilda in Rome. She undergoes a cycle of despair similar to Donatello's. Her splendid isolation destroyed by her brush with sin, she loses both the sympathy she once had for the old masters and her ability as a copyist. Searching for someone to share what she feels is guilty knowledge, she begins to long for Kenyon's affection. He arrives just after she had eased her soul by confession in St. Peter's, and she begins to show some stirrings of love for him. Hilda starts to regret her brusque treatment of Miriam, who had come to her in need of help. She is beginning to share in the common emotions of love and pity, and she is spirited away by the plot machinery to finish her transformation.

The next section, Chapters XLIII to XLIX, covers the period of Hilda's disappearance and centers on Kenyon. Before he realizes that Hilda is missing, he meets Miriam and Donatello, and he cannot understand why they should risk their happiness by returning to Rome, although he can see Donatello's penitent's costume. Discovering that Hilda is really gone, he becomes more and more worried, realizing at last that she is not the idealized woman he had thought, but an inexperienced girl who might have encountered numberless accidents in Rome. Concerned only for Hilda, he cannot even develop a real interest in a newly discovered Venus, and Hawthorne comments, "He could hardly, we fear, be reckoned a consummate artist, because there was something dearer to him than his art" (p. 834). Meeting Miriam and Donatello again, he fails to understand them or the apparent connection between their surrender and Hilda's release. When Miriam poses the question of the Fortunate Fall—that sin may be a necessary means for salvation—he can neither refute nor reject it, but he refuses to admit that man has the right to even consider such an idea. "It is too dangerous, Miriam! I cannot follow you. . . . Mortal man has no right to tread on the ground where you now set your feet" (p. 840). He doesn't even notice the arrest of Miriam and Donatello at the moment of Hilda's reappearance. Concerned solely with his beloved, Kenyon can no longer feel the claims of art or of wider or deeper human sympathy.

The last chapter bears the same title as the first, "Miriam, Hilda, Kenyon, Donatello." It considers the probable fates of the two couples. Hilda and Kenyon are to become a happily married New England pair. He will never be a "consummate artist," but will probably be a respected carver of buttonholes. When he offers Hilda Miriam's idea of the Fortunate Fall, she is shocked and disgusted, and they reject it in favor of happy orthodoxy.

What will become of Miriam and Donatello is left in mystery, but it is almost certain that their lives will contain little of ordinary human happiness. Unlike Hilda and Kenyon, however, they have not been afraid to look deep into human nature, no matter how strange and unsettling the things they see. So each couple's story illustrates one of Hawthorne's alternatives: Hilda and Kenyon find earthly happiness at the cost of losing profound insight and the chance of creating great art; Miriam and Donatello gain profound insight at the cost of happiness.

Seen in this perspective, the careful structure of the novel is

evident. The murder of the model is the pivotal event. The three
sections before it presented the characters, their relationships, and
the buildup of emotional tension which precipitated the murder.
The four sections following show the changes brought about by it,
progressing from the most immediately concerned to the farthest
removed. Each character underwent a profound change, but the
transformations were as various as the characters themselves.

The novel's content is complex, and so, necessarily, is its form.
The structure is complex, but it is a structure and not the chaos it
has so often been called.

Sheldon W. Liebman

The Design of
The Marble Faun

In *The Marble Faun*, Hawthorne's last complete novel, the
reader is confronted with a mass of images, symbols, and allusions far more diverse and extensive than those in the earlier
novels. Consequently, as Merle E. Brown mentions, this novel has
been subjected to "a plethora of interpretations," no single one
of which is especially satisfactory.[1] Brown is right in assuming
that it is Hawthorne's design or structure which must be delineated
before Hawthorne's ethics and metaphysics can be defined and his
artistic accomplishment appreciated.

The most significant error that many critics of *The Marble
Faun* have made is in first taking Hawthorne at face value and
in then demanding conclusions from him in absolute terms.
One of Hawthorne's most effective techniques is simply to suggest *both* black and white: to draw near to a conclusion, retreat, and propose another. Moreover, Hawthorne speaks through
no single character and proposes as ideal no particular way-of-life.
A valid interpretation cannot be based upon *what* Kenyon says or

Reprinted from *New England Quarterly*, XL (March, 1967), 61–78, by
permission of the *New England Quarterly* and the author.
[1] "The Structure of *The Marble Faun*," *American Literature*, XXVIII, 302
(Nov., 1956).

what Miriam says or even upon *what* Hawthorne says. Rather, the reader derives meaning from the work of art by treating Hawthorne as an artist not as a moralist or a prophet.

Critics have also tended to isolate a single aspect of *The Marble Faun* and have then rested their view of the novel entirely upon that element alone. Brown, again, is a case-in-point, for he concentrates solely on Hawthorne's characterizations and character developments, leaving untouched the artist's intricate imagery and symbolization. The novel obviously has a great deal to do with the Fall myth, for example, yet Brown is forced to disregard it. Hawthorne can speak as an artist only through the *whole* novel, only through the *sum* of ostensibly irreconcilable parts. My object will be to examine a few of these "parts"—character, scene, allusion, and metaphor—and to find their patterns and relationships. My assumption is that when specific qualities of scene or character are emphasized (by either contrast or repetition, or both) a motif is established which must be reconciled with other motifs. I shall try to show that in *The Marble Faun*, all these culminate in a single "structural" motif: a complex but total pattern of symbols, metaphors, images, and symbolic actions; a pattern which recurs frequently and regularly in the novel, and which provides a framework and unity for the action.[2]

I

Probably the most obvious motif of Hawthorne's *The Marble Faun* is the Fall myth. Eden and Paradise are mentioned over and over again, and the similarity between Donatello and Miriam, on the one hand, and Adam and Eve, on the other, is at least implicit in the novel.

Hawthorne builds Donatello's character on the statue of the Faun, who is a representative of mankind "in its innocent childhood; before sin, sorrow, or morality itself had ever been thought of." [3] Kenyon first suggests the similarities between Donatello and the Faun; and Hilda ("whose perception of form and expression were wonderfully clear and delicate") agrees, at least, that "the

---

[2] "The novel is able to express the most profound ideas, but, because of the nature of this medium, these will lie implicitly in the conjunction of the events that are bodied forth. The ideas in a novel are largely for the reader's inference, his inference of the principles by which the happenings in the book are related to each other" (Dorothy Van Ghent, *The English Novel: Form and Function* [New York, 1961], p. 6).

[3] *The Marble Faun, The Complete Works of Nathaniel Hawthorne* (Boston, 1896), VI, 27. Subsequent references are to this edition.

resemblance is very close, and very strange." Donatello himself is outside the law, a perfect blend of nature and art. In the catacombs he expresses his "repugnance" at anything associated with death. Like Adam, he is a daylight creature, afraid of the dark, yet convinced of his own immortality: "Why should it have any end? How long! Forever, forever, forever!" [4]

Miriam is an "Eve" character more by action than by description. Bewitching and "Oriental," she is of mysterious origins, but we learn little of her. Only her resemblance to Kenyon's statue of Cleopatra gives us a more precise hint of her character—the same method which Hawthorne uses with Donatello. Yet Miriam's role as temptress is repeated sufficiently to give her the identity of Eve. Donatello would never have entered the catacombs except that Miriam's "attractive influence alone had enticed him into that gloomy region." [5] Later, Miriam beckons Donatello into the shadowy corner of her room. Finally, she lures him out of his innocence into the world of sin, into the darkest corner of darkness, when he heaves the body of the spectre from Traitor's Leap.

Together, Miriam and Donatello are "the beautiful man, the beautiful woman, united forever..." [6] by a crime which severs Donatello from his innocent past and, significantly, makes him Miriam's equal. Milton's Eve too, felt it necessary to make Adam share her guilt so that they should be equal:

> Thou therefore also taste, that equal Lot
> May joyne us, equal Joy, as equal Love;
> Least thou not tasting, different degree
> Disjoyne us, and I then too late renounce
> Deitie for thee, when Fate will not permit. [7]

---

[4] *The Marble Faun,* 102. Brown distinguishes between Donatello as faun and Donatello as Adam. The idea that *The Marble Faun* is a retelling of the Fall, says Brown, "can be sustained only if it is decided that before the murder Donatello was in exactly the state Adam was in before the Fall.... Donatello (however) is made to appear much more like a faun than like Adam" and is in "a different predicament from Adam's." What must be emphasized, however (as it is by Brown), is that Donatello's most significant experience is his transformation. The same sequence of events—innocence, rebellion, dissociation—is experienced by both Adam and Donatello. The latter is at least the "new" Adam, that is, innocence reborn in a new environment. In some sense, at least, Hawthorne's novel is the story of the Fall.
[5] *The Marble Faun,* 41.
[6] *The Marble Faun,* 370.
[7] *Paradise Lost,* IX, 886–890, in *Restoration and Augustan Poets,* edited by W. H. Auden and N. H. Pearson (New York, 1957).

After drinking a "marriage" toast at the Trevi Fountain which is blessed by the spectre's presence, Miriam and Donatello consummate a "union that consists in guilt." They are then "shut out of heaven" (Hilda's presence), new members of the Brotherhood of Evil, forever separated from God and the angels, as are Milton's Adam and Eve: "How shall I behold the face/Henceforth of God or Angel, earst with joy/And rapture so oft beheld?" [8]

Hawthorne alludes specifically to the Paradise of Adam and Eve several times in the novel. The Borghese Garden "is like Eden in its loveliness; like Eden, too, in the fatal spell that removes it beyond the scope of man's actual possessions." [9] It is the scene of Miriam's and Donatello's last dance of innocence, the perfection of which is marred only by the intrusion of the spectre:

> In due time, some mortal, whom they reverence too highly, is commissioned by Providence to teach them this direful lesson; he perpetrates a sin; and Adam falls anew, and Paradise, here to fore in unfaded bloom is lost again, and closed forever, with the fiery swords gleaming at its gates. [10]

Not only are Miriam and Donatello stained with the blood of murder, but so, too, is Hilda, for "every crime destroys more Edens than our own." [11]

Hawthorne's vision of the "fortunate fall" is much the same as Milton's. In *Areopagitica*, the poet sets forth the argument which was later to appear in *Paradise Lost*, that good is nothing without the existence of Evil:

> Many there be who complain of divine providence for suffering Adam to transgress; foolish tongues! When God gave him reason, he gave him freedom to choose, for reason is but choosing.... God therefore left him free, set before him a provoking object, ever almost in his eyes; herein consisted his merit, herein the right of his reward, the praise of his abstinence. [12]

Miriam, too, justifying the ways of God to man, considers the existence of evil on similar terms:

---

[8] *Paradise Lost*, IX, 1084–1086.
[9] *The Marble Faun*, 93.
[10] *The Marble Faun*, 238.
[11] *The Marble Faun*, 247.
[12] *Areopagitica* in *Seventeenth Century Prose and Poetry*, edited by A. M. Witherspoon and F. J. Warnke (New York, 1963), 405.

The story of the fall of man! Is it not repeated in our romance of
Monte Beni? And may we follow the analogy yet further? Was
that very sin,—into which Adam precipitated himself and all his
race,—was it the destined means by which, over a long pathway of
toil and sorrow, we are to attain a higher, brighter and profounder
happiness, than our lost birthright gave? Will not this idea account
for the permitted existence of sin, as no other theory can? [13]

But not only in ideas and action are *The Marble Faun* and
Paradise Lost alike, for even in tone, Milton and Hawthorne
are at one. Compare the following two passages, the first, Kenyon's impression of the whole experience of Donatello and Miriam,
the second, Milton's view of the sinners' exit from Paradise:

[Miriam], too, like Donatello, had reached a wayside paradise, in
their mysterious life-journey, where they both threw down the
burden of the before and after.... Today, Donatello was the Sylvan Faun; today, Miriam was his fit companion, a Nymph of
grove or fountain; tomorrow,—a remorseful man and woman,
linked by a marriage-bond of crime, they would set forth towards
an inevitable goal.[14]

> Some natural tears they drop'd, but wip'd them soon;
> The world was all before them, where to choose
> Their place of rest, and Providence their guide;
> They hand in hand with wand'ring steps and slow,
> Through Eden took their solitarie way.[15]

Both have the same sense of melancholy, the same feeling of
mixed joy and despair. Hawthorne's, surely, is the traditional
vision of the "fortunate fall," which runs through Milton, Pope,
Wordsworth, Tennyson, and Camus, the vision of good and evil,
life and death gripped in one poetic fist.[16]

Certainly the Fall myth is an integral part of *The Marble
Faun*. Though central to the action of the novel, however, the
story of Adam and Eve is not its structural motif. Too much
action lies outside the framework of the myth. The first problem that presents itself in this context is the fact that Hawthorne's

---

13 *The Marble Faun*, 491.
14 *The Marble Faun*, 492.
15 *Paradise Lost*, XI, 650–654.
16 The problem of "the Fall" is satisfactorily settled by Sidney P. Moss, who
states that "the doctrine of the fortunate fall is deliberately left unresolved . . ." ("The Problem of Theme in *The Marble Faun*," *Nineteenth
Century Fiction*, XVIII, 399 [March, 1964]).

retelling of the Fall ends at the murder scene, and appears only intermittently throughout the rest of the novel. From this point on, the novel alternately concentrates its focus on Donatello, on Hilda, and, finally, on Kenyon. Although the relationship between Donatello and Miriam is significant until the end, it is subordinate to the relationship between Kenyon and Hilda, after Chapter XXXV.

The second problem is the relationship Hilda and Kenyon bear to Miriam and Donatello. If the latter are Adam and Eve, who, then, is Hilda? She does come close to being something of a God-figure or, at least, an angel. Kenyon, the other half of the problem, could possibly fit into a Biblical scheme as a priest (Hawthorne describes sculptors as a priesthood). He administers sympathy to Donatello and even effects the latter's reunion with Miriam. In the final analysis, however, the Fall myth forms a cluster of allusions which constitute an important motif in the novel, but which does not set the pace and frame the action of the work as a whole.[17]

II

A second possibility is suggested in Merle Brown's study of *The Marble Faun*. Brown pursues the thesis that the design of the novel is based on its British publication title: *Transformation*. He points out that each character experiences a sequence of actions which leads him from innocence to knowledge of evil and, finally, to some sort of reconciliation. The pattern—innocence, experience or knowledge of evil, isolation, pilgrimage, return—is followed by Miriam, Donatello, Hilda, and Kenyon, successively.

However, even though Brown makes allowances in the case of Hilda (she is never *completely* reconciled to the "fact" of evil), his interpretation does not suffice. Rather than showing similarities in the development of each character, the transformation motif sharpens the differences in their personalities.

Hilda changes very little. She rejects Miriam in Chapter XXIII and never has the opportunity to show any modification in her attitude toward her "evil" friend. In the first place (to Brown), transformation implies some sort of development from

---

[17] The conclusion of Sidney P. Moss that "the romance is a modern retelling of the Genesis story," is therefore not entirely correct. As I have said, the Fall myth is *a* theme, not *the* theme.

lower to higher consciousness, the adjustment the ego makes to the challenge of the real world. This change involves growth of aware- ness, expansion of consciousness, rather than constriction or inhi- bition. Rather than permit the knowledge of evil to enter her conscious mind, Hilda pushes it out of her memory:

> Hilda, as is sometimes the case with persons whose delicate organi- zation requires a peculiar safeguard, had *an elastic faculty of throwing off such recollections as would be too painful for en- durance.* The first shock of Donatello's and Miriam's crime had, indeed, broken through the frail defense of this voluntary forget- fulness; but, once enabled *to relieve herself of the ponderous an- guish* over which she had so long brooded, she had practiced a *subtile watchfulness in preventing its return.*[18]

It is not difficult to see the similarities between Hilda's psy- chological defense against anxiety and Freud's concept of re- pression. Hilda is able to keep peace-of-mind only at the cost of insight and understanding. "There is, I believe, only one right and one wrong," she says,

> and I do not understand, and may God keep me from understand- ing, how two things so totally unlike can be mistaken for one an- other; nor how two mortal foes, as Right and Wrong surely are, can work together in the same deed. This is my faith; and I should be led astray, if you could persuade me to give it up.[19]

Unlike Kenyon, Hilda cannot even attempt to reconcile good and evil, and Hawthorne takes pains to point out the fact. That she manages to come down from her heavenly tower and marry Kenyon does not indicate any significant alteration in her one-sided personality. Hilda remains, in Milton's words, a woman of "fugitive and cloistered virtue, unexercised and un- breathed, that never sallies out and sees her adversary, but slinks out of the race, where the immortal garland is to be run for, not without dust and heat." [20]

Since Miriam is associated with past guilt and sin as early as Chapter III, we should expect her to change little in reference to knowledge of evil. Rather, the effect of her partnership in

---

[18] *The Marble Faun,* 435. Italics mine.
[19] *The Marble Faun,* 437.
[20] *Seventeenth Century Prose and Poetry,* 402.

the murder serves to bring her back to humanity, in that she gains a comrade in sin and no longer needs to experience the terror of loneliness.

Brown believes that Miriam, early in the novel, "cannot endure . . . the idea that there is any evil in herself." Yet Miriam identifies herself strongly with Hilda's painted Beatrice Cenci. She understands Beatrice's plight simply because the two have had similar experiences. If Brown's estimate of Miriam is correct, we should expect her to maintain Beatrice's innocence which, in fact, she controverts. Neither is it true that "suddenly [after the murder] her vision penetrates the facade of ordinary life," and that she "suddenly" sees the bond between herself and all sinners. In the first place, Miriam's very self-identification with Beatrice is a pre-murder recognition of this bond and, secondly, she is fairly worldly wise even from the beginning of the novel.

Neither Hilda nor Miriam changes, but each sets the other in high relief. Whereas for Milton they would represent the right and wrong attitudes toward good and evil, for Hawthorne they are simply different attitudes; and, whether right or wrong, they are as much a part of the real world as good and evil, and equally necessary and understandable.

In much the same way, Kenyon opposes Donatello; the latter is "Miriam-ized," the former "Hilda-ized." Donatello moves from ignorance to understanding (Miriam's point-of-view) while Kenyon moves from relative understanding to relative ignorance (Hilda's point-of-view). Kenyon *does* change, but in a direction opposite to that of transformation, according to Brown's definitions. Early in the novel, Kenyon is inquisitive, unwilling to respect the "secrets of the unknown." He wants to know whether or not Donatello is, in fact, a Faun. Hilda castigates "this inclination, which most people have, to explain away the wonder and mystery out of everything." [21] In spite of Hilda's disparaging remarks, however, Kenyon continues to inquire. Unlike Hilda, who breaks off her friendship with Miriam after the murder, Kenyon pursues Donatello and displays, in the course of their relationship, an almost indefatigable curiosity and sympathy. Eventually, though, in turning this interest from Donatello and Miriam to Hilda, he loses contact with the dilemma of the two guilty ones. In the meeting on the Campagna, Kenyon is strikingly unsympathetic to the lovers' doom, in his impatience to see Hilda. Finally he bows

---

[21] *The Marble Faun,* 128.

to Hilda's demand that he "hush" and forget his Miltonic justification of the Fall. "Forgive me, Hilda," he replies, ". . . O Hilda, guide me home!" [22]

To sum up, "transformation" is not quite satisfactory as a structural motif, simply because Miriam and Hilda are never actually transformed. Many of Brown's ideas are pertinent and valid, but we must conclude with Kenyon that "it is the spectator's mood that transfigures the Transfiguration itself." [23]

III

The structure of the novel is based on neither the myth motif nor the explicit thematic motif. Although both of these narrow the focus of the story, neither provides a complete framework for the action. It is a short step, of course, from the Fall myth to the "transformation" idea. The two are compatible in that the innocence-experience development is basic to each. Moreover, implicit in both motifs is the idea of duality or ambivalence. First, the Fall myth suggests the necessity of knowledge of both good and evil, that existence is nothing if it does not recognize the "two-ness" of things. Second, as we have seen, the certainty of Donatello's transformation sets up an opposition between characters and between pairs of characters.

Most of the chapters are, in fact, structured on oppositions between images, ideas, and time and place.[24] Chapter I establishes three ambivalences which are continued in subsequent chapters: [25] (1) innocence and evil (the statue of the child), (2) past and present (Rome), and (3) myth and reality (the Faun and Donatello). Chapter II continues to play myth against reality, but recalls innocence-evil and past-present in opposing Donatello and the Dying Gladiator. By comparing Donatello to the spectre in Chapter IV, Hawthorne sets light against dark, dance against

---

[22] *The Marble Faun*, 520.

[23] *The Marble Faun*, 31.

[24] Richard H. Fogle sums up the oppositional structure as "complexity vs. simplicity" in his *Hawthorne's Fiction: The Light and the Dark* (Norman, 1952), 164 ff. Gary J. Scrimgeour also examines Hawthorne's use of opposites in his article, *"The Marble Faun: Hawthorne's Faery Land," American Literature*, XXXVI, 271–287 (Nov., 1964).

[25] Hawthorne's universe of forces and qualities is ambivalent, not simply "ambiguous" as Professor Waggoner maintains. Each element has meaning only in terms of its opposite. Professor Waggoner does, however, see Hawthorne's material as *archetypal*. It seems to me that the word "ambiguous" is a little misleading. See Waggoner's "Introduction," *Nathaniel Hawthorne: Selected Tales and Sketches* (New York, 1960), xxi–xii.

death. It is important to notice that each opposition emanates from a unit (such as Rome or the statue of the child) and that the obviously opposing forces are united when they do not develop from a unit (such as Donatello and the spectre; for all the differences between them, both are bewitched by Miriam and both "haunt her footsteps" [26]). In Chapter VI, Miriam (an unknown Oriental, shadowy and mysterious) opposes Hilda (a known westerner, neither shadowy nor mysterious). Chapter VIII shows the life-and-death aspects of the Borghese Gardens. Chapter XIII investigates the ambivalence of Rome; is it an illusion (with "transient, visionary structures") or is it real ("no land of dreams but the broadest page of history")? Two symbols, the skull (death) and the shrub (life), make up the ambivalence in Chapter XXVIII. Chapter XXXV shows two sides of Perugia: Pope Julius opposes the petty tumult of the market place; the sunny hilltop opposes the cavernous streets plunging into darkness. These are just a few of the ambivalences in which the novel abounds.

In addition to the oppositional structure *within* each chapter is the *pattern* of those chapters, that is, the relations which the chapters bear to each other. Chapters I, VI, XIII, XVIII, XXIII, XXVIII, and XXXV are situated in particularly high places. In each of these chapters, Hawthorne emphasizes (1) the distinction between ideal and real, in terms of high and low, and (2) the uniqueness of the view. In all these instances, a character looks out from a particularly small or narrow place to the broad expanse of rooftops or countryside. Usually, someone sees the *whole* city or *whole* countryside from a narrow parapet or through a window. Yet he sees only roofs, domes, sunny reflections, stars. The view is vast yet specifically limited in breadth (framed by hills) and, more especially, limited in intensity and depth. It is necessary to "ascend" to truth, but only figuratively speaking. Reality lies beneath the roofs, below the domes, "a mighty subterrannean lake of gore, right beneath our feet." [27]

Alternate scenes in *The Marble Faun* take place "beneath our feet" in Chapters III, VIII, XVII, XXI, XXV, and XXXII. The catacombs, Borghese Gardens, Colosseum, Capuchin cemetery, and Donatello's decayed saloon are all either beneath the ground or in enclosed areas. Certain images recur in these chapters, also,

---

[26] Darrel Abel provides elaborate support for the juxtaposition of Donatello and the Spectre in his article, "A Masque of Love and Death," *University of Toronto Quarterly,* XXIII, 14–15 (March, 1953).
[27] *The Marble Faun,* 193.

which set them in opposition to the Capitoline Museum, Hilda's Room, the Pincian Hill, Donatello's Tower, the Tarpeian Rock, and the hilltop city, Perugia; all elevated, all above reality, all *centrifugal* in vision. The principal similarity among the "low" chapters is their association with death. The catacombs are, in fact, tombs with death niches lining the walls. The Borghese Gardens is a scene not only of mirth but also of disease: "The final charm is bestowed by the malaria." [28] The Colosseum is a kind of tomb for the Dying Gladiator. The Capuchin cemetery is a tomb constructed of the bones of long-dead monks. All of these chapters are funereal, illuminated by diffused sunlight, torches, or moonlight. They are scenes of decay consecrated by death; shadowy, dreamy, and grotesque. Nearly every scene is dominated by a circle which encloses the action and focuses attention on the center: "the circular chapel" of the catacombs, "the wild ring of mirth" in the "Sylvan Dance," the circular Colosseum, the "wreath of dancing figures" which covers the walls of Donatello's saloon, and the journey of Donatello back to Rome which completes the circle of his development. The vision of these chapters is *centripetal*.

The chapters of *The Marble Faun* thus follow a distinct pattern. The characters ascend and delve, move from high to low, from tower to circle. By itself, this movement means little. Seen in the context of the other motifs, however, it is a comment on the journey-of-life as are the other motifs, and is, in fact, a variation and extension of the Fall and transformation motifs:

> Every human life, *if it ascends to truth or delves down to reality,* must undergo a similar change . . . how ill prepared he stood, on this old battle-field of the world, to fight with such an inevitable foe as mortal calamity, and sin for its stronger ally.[29]

Yet, although this regular movement sets a definite rhythm for the action, the high-low motif ends at Chapter XXXV. Subsequent chapters are no longer distinguished by ascent and descent. So, again, this motif does not frame the action of the novel.

IV

An important metaphor of *The Marble Faun* is the comparison of Rome to a dead body. Rome is described as a grave in Chapters

---

[28] *The Marble Faun,* 92.
[29] *The Marble Faun,* 302–303. Italics mine.

II and XII. Rome is a corpse in Chapters XII, XVI, and XXXVI.
The Dying Gladiator appears in Chapters I and II as well as in
the Colosseum scene, in which a black cross marks the spot of
a gladiator's death at the *central* point of the Colosseum, just as
Rome is the *center* of a deadly circle in Chapter XXIV. Extending
the "dead body" metaphor, Hawthorne describes Miriam's and
the spectre's meeting-place as "the bowels of the earth." Yet,
too, Rome is the "eternal city," center of life as well as death.

Two kinds of action recur with sufficient frequency and reg-
ularity to take on *symbolic* significance. Each of the "low chapters" is a scene of either a dance or a pilgrimage. The journey
to the catacombs is a kind of pilgrimage for the major characters,
since it is a visit to shrines and tombs. This scene foreshadows
subsequent individual pilgrimages. The spectre kneels at every
shrine in the Colosseum, and is, in the eyes of the spectators, a
"pilgrim." Miriam's pilgrimage takes place at the Capuchin cemetery, a scene of shrines and tombs. As a penance, she gives the
sacristan money, "an amount that made his eyes open wide and
glisten." [30] Donatello's pilgrimage takes place on the road back
to Rome, when he stops at shrines along the way: "Beholding
these consecrated stations, the idea seemed to strike Donatello
of converting the otherwise aimless journey into a penitential
pilgrimage." [31] Hilda, too, in her loneliness, "now entered upon
another pilgrimage among these altars and shrines" [32] of the
churches of Rome. Kenyon's walk on the Campagna is a pilgrimage
of sorts. He is alone, searching among "the tombs of the Appian
Way," for word of Hilda or some sign of her existence. The visit
to the Pantheon by Kenyon, Miriam, and Hilda in Chapter L is
the final pilgrimage and effectively encloses the novel in a definite
frame. The movement is from the "circular chapel" of the catacombs to the "great circle" of the Pantheon, from darkness to
light, from unconsciousness to consciousness.

The dance motif appears in Chapters II, V, X, XXV, and
XLVIII. Donatello dances around the Dying Gladiator in the
Capitoline Museum. Later, he dances in Miriam's room "like
an incarnate spirit of jollity." [33] In the Borghese Gardens, both
Miriam and Donatello join in a "sylvan dance" to which the
others are soon attracted "as if they were all gone mad with

---

[30] *The Marble Faun,* 228.
[31] *The Marble Faun,* 341.
[32] *The Marble Faun,* 394.
[33] *The Marble Faun,* 64.

jollity." [34] The shadowy saloon at Donatello's palace is covered with frescoes of wildly dancing figures. Finally, the carnival at Rome caps the dance motif with a mass celebration. As the ingenuous Donatello once danced around the Dying Gladiator, so, now, Rome dances around Donatello, the gladiator reborn "on the battlefield of the world."

The question now remains: what do these elements of the novel have to do with each other? The setting is a massive corpse, Rome, dead but eternal, around which the characters either dance in pageantry or march in penitence. The symbol which ties these together—dance, pilgrimage, and corpse—is the *sarcophagus*,

> where, as often as any other device, a festive procession mocks the ashes and white bones that are treasured up within. You might take it for a marriage-pageant; but after a while, if you look at these merry-makers, following them from end to end of the marble coffin, you doubt whether the gay movement is leading them to a happy close. [35]

This image recurs again and again both explicitly and implicitly throughout the novel. It begins simply as a casual allusion in Hawthorne's description of the sculpture room at the Capitoline Museum:

> And here, in this sarcophagus, the exquisitely carved figures might assume life, and chase one another round its verge with that wild merriment which is so strangely represented on those old burial coffers: though still with some subtle allusion to death, carefully veiled, but forever peeping forth amid emblems of mirth and riot.[36]

After this, in Chapter X, the sarcophagus becomes a metaphor for the sylvan dance (quoted above). In Chapter XVII, in which the scene is the tomb-like Colosseum, Hawthorne describes the strange combination of dancing maidens and a pilgrim, simultaneously expressing themselves; one in mirth, the other in penitence. "For in Italy," he explains, "religion jostles along side by side with business and sport, after a fashion of its own, and people are accustomed to kneel down and pray, or see others

---

[34] *The Marble Faun*, 108.
[35] *The Marble Faun*, 110.
[36] *The Marble Faun*, 32.

praying, between two fits of merriment, or between two sins." [37]
And is not this the sarcophagus scene again? Every thirty or forty
pages, the motif reappears, gaining momentum and significance
as the multiple associations unravel themselves. Chapter XXV
pursues the same paradox of "the grim identity between gay
things and sorrowful ones. Only give them a little time, and they
turn out to be just alike!" [38] Donatello peruses the frescoes of his
ancient saloon, finding that "one of the figures ... was repeated
many times over in the groups upon the wall and ceiling," in
much the same way that the reader follows the perplexing pattern
of the sarcophagus. "It [one of the figures] formed the principal
link of an allegory," Hawthorne remarks,

> by which (as often the case in such pictorial designs) the whole
> series of frescoes were bound together, but which it would be im-
> possible, or, at least, very wearisome to unravel. The sculptor's
> eyes took a similar direction, and soon began to trace through the
> vicissitudes—once gay, now sombre—in which the old artist had
> involved it, the same individual figure. [39]

Here, Hawthorne almost seems to be describing his own method.
For Donatello is, in fact, the central figure in the pattern, alternately dancing and pilgrimaging. But where does the journey
lead? It seems to be aimless, yet, "if you look closely into the
matter, it will be seen that whatever appears most vagrant, and
utterly purposeless, turns out, in the end, to have been impelled
the most surely on a preordained and unswerving track. [40] For
all this, however, the image remains ambivalent. The only thing
we can be sure of is that man is engaged in a perpetual search for
happiness, to which Hawthorne answers, "How exceedingly absurd!" [41]

The final sarcophagus scene is the carnival (Chapter XLVIII),
which is literally a marriage pageant for Kenyon and Hilda, and
a funeral march for Donatello and Miriam. The grotesque array
of masks and confetti is Hawthorne's closing comment on the
human comedy: "a sympathy of nonsense; a true and genial
brotherhood and sisterhood, based on the honest purpose—and

---

[37] *The Marble Faun*, 184.
[38] *The Marble Faun*, 261.
[39] *The Marble Faun*, 263.
[40] *The Marble Faun*, 333.
[41] *The Marble Faun*, 466.

a wise one, too—of being foolish, all together. The sport of mankind, like its deepest earnest, is a battle. . . ." [42]

The sarcophagus image seems, at first, a striking but uncharacteristic vehicle for Hawthorne's vision of life. Yet, after all, for the man who once imagined life as a "festal or funereal procession," [43] what metaphor could be more appropriate? Moreover, the juxtaposition of marriage and death in Hawthorne's works is not confined only to *The Marble Faun*.[44] The theme characterized by the sarcophagus scene is a motif, almost an obsession, in both *Twice Told Tales* and *Mosses from an Old Manse*. It is an artistic triumph in *The Marble Faun*.[45]

Unlike the motifs examined earlier, the elements which combine to make up the sarcophagus motif provide a framework for the entire novel. Every action can be seen as one side or the other of the "utterly inscrutable" ways of Providence, as portrayed in the strange patterns of a marble casket. As Gary J. Scrimgeour has noted, "Throughout all [Hawthorne's] romances, one is conscious that the events Hawthorne describes are always struggling out of the confines of the time in which they are happening into a plane where they are the reenactment of an eternally recurring event." [46]

---

[42] *The Marble Faun*, 407.

[43] "The Procession of Life," *Mosses from an Old Manse, Works,* II, 235. Leading the journey is the Chief Marshal, Death. Hawthorne continues, "Who else could assume the guidance of a procession that comprehends all humanity . . ." (251).

[44] For example, Dr. Heidegger's intended bride had died on the bridal evening. In "Howe's Masquerade" a funeral procession enters amid the festivities of a masked ball. The partners to a wedding ceremony in "The Wedding Knell" are leaders, respectively, of a marriage pageant and of a funeral procession. The groom summons his bride to be married and then to die. It is the irony of the vision which strikes Hawthorne when he says, "The whole scene expressed, by the strongest imagery, the vain struggle of the gilded vanities of this world, when opposed to age, infirmity, sorrow, and death" (*Twice Told Tales, Works,* I, 49). See also "The Lily's Quest" in the same volume.

[45] Mr. Abel states: "The motif of life as a never ending dance of sinister and mirthful figures is reiterated in the visible properties which surround the characters in [Hawthorne's] story: the procession of life represented on vases and sarcophagi, friezes and murals, in the grotesqueries of the Carnival, in funeral ceremonies and the ritual practices of monks and penitents, in the daily bustle of Roman streets, and the festivity and frolic of country life." *University of Toronto Quarterly,* XXIII, 24.

[46] Mr. Scrimgeour sees the journey as a kind of unending ramble: "Each ramble also places the events in their proper perspective as part of the marble of time, makes us see them as universal and eternal rather than romantic and unique, extends them backwards through the course of history (Christian, classical, pagan) so that they are repeated in an unbroken chain back to Arcadia and forward to—what?" *American Literature,* XXXVI, 284 (Nov., 1964).

Structurally, the sarcophagus is a catch-all for the other motifs of the novel. It is a catacomb, at first, revealing death and despair; the Campagna, an excavated catacomb, later, revealing life and hope. Whereas the Fall myth and the "transformation" motifs are, respectively, moral and psychological justifications of human experience, the sarcophagus is a metaphor for the life-journey viewed almost scientifically, without rationale and outside any ideological construct. Thus, Miriam suffers and Donatello dies, not because they are "evil," but because it is the nature of the *experienced* to suffer and die. Similarly, Hilda lives on and thrives not because she is "good," but because it is the nature of the innocent to live and thrive. This paradox of life and death pervades *The Marble Faun* from beginning to end, and Hawthorne's final comment is that life is both absurd and pathetic, both meaningful and meaningless. Hawthorne's is a universe in equipoise with mankind journeying through, unsure of its intentions, uncertain about its destiny.

"It is not his habit to come to ultimate conclusions" says Professor Fogle of Hawthorne,[47] and certainly no conclusion is necessary. Hawthorne was more scientist than prophet, more analyst than visionary.[48] "There is no synthesis in Hawthorne's thinking, only thesis and antithesis in balance."[49] Yet there *is* synthesis in Hawthorne's art: the Fall of man, transformation, the ironies of unconsciousness and consciousness, all are reconciled and related by the intertwinings of Hawthorne's artistry. We see them, finally, as versions of the same story, a story which was, to Hawthorne, a source (perhaps the only source) of our understanding of the uniquely human in man's experience. As he says in "David Swan":

We can be but partially acquainted even with the events which actually influence our course through life, and our final destiny. There are innumerable other events—if such they may be called— which come close upon us, yet pass away without actual results, or even betraying their near approach, by the reflection of any light or shadow across our minds. Could we know all the vicissitudes of our fortunes, life would be too full of hope and fear, exultation or disappointment, to afford us a single hour of true serenity.[50]

[47] R. H. Fogle, *Hawthorne's Fiction,* 168.
[48] This point is also made by Mr. Scrimgeour who calls Hawthorne "more wise than didactic."
[49] Fogle, 192.
[50] *Twice-Told Tales, Works,* I, 211.

F. O. Matthiessen

[The Context of
"The Fortunate Fall"]

... It seems strange that so many critics have taken out of its context one of Miriam's speculations near the end of the book, in order to assert that Hawthorne's theme here is that the fall of man was really his rise. She argues to Kenyon that since Donatello's crime seems to have been the means of educating his simple nature to a level of feeling and intelligence that it would not have reached under any other discipline, may it not be that Adam's sin 'was the destined means by which, over a long pathway of toil and sorrow, we are to attain a higher, brighter, and profounder happiness than any our lost birthright gave? Will not this idea account for the permitted existence of sin, as no other theory can?' 'O felix culpa,' declares the Exultet for the Holy Saturday Mass, 'quae talem et tantum meruit habere redemptorem.'

But hardly more than the Church does Hawthorne hold this to be the whole truth. Miriam herself trembles at these irrepressible thoughts on regeneration through sin. Hawthorne declares that Kenyon 'rightly felt' them to be too perilous. But the novelist did not need to make this open comment, for the whole course of his action bears out that hardly more than Milton was he 'of the Devil's party without knowing it.' That comment on *Paradise Lost* was made by the greatest of the English romantics, Blake, and was subscribed to by Shelley in his equal fascination with the character of Lucifer. But what this interpretation ignores is the cumulative effect of the whole poem, the gradual decay and final degradation of the former Prince of Heaven, as the consequences of his fall from grace work themselves out inevitably in debasing his nature.

In comparable fashion, an understanding of *The Marble Faun* depends on being aware of the work as a whole. We must not overlook the circumstances in which Miriam's speculation occurs, for it is during the Roman Carnival, with its vestiges of the old pagan rite of spring. Miriam and Donatello have seized on the

From *American Renaissance*, pp. 310–12. Copyright 1941 by Oxford University Press, Inc. Reprinted by permission.

disguise of a masquerade for a moment of gay forgetfulness of their destiny. But when they encounter Kenyon, this is brought again, unavoidably, to the fore. It strikes the sculptor that these two have reached 'a wayside paradise,' but to-morrow—and here the analogy with the closing lines of *Paradise Lost* could hardly be more marked—'a remorseful man and woman, linked by a marriage-bond of crime, they would set forth towards an inevitable goal.' [1] Nor is that goal left shrouded in any doubt, for it is made explicit at the end that her life is to be spent in penitence, his in prison.

Even here, in his one diffuse handling of the European scene, and in spite of what Eliot has called 'all its Walter Scott-Mysteries of Udolpho upholstery,' Hawthorne has again established a world of solid moral values. It is based on a conception of man as a being radically imperfect, destined to struggle through a long labyrinth of error, and to suffer harsh and cruel shocks. The contrast with the one-way optimism of most of Hawthorne's contemporaries could hardly be more striking, and runs parallel to the estimate that Perry Miller has made of the value of the Puritans for us to-day. . . .

---

[1] The romantic interpretation generally remembers, as an augury of happiness, this line:

> The world was all before them where to choose.

It neglects the fact that Adam and Eve have just been driven out of Paradise, and that the following and final lines destroy any suggestion of the joy of the open road:

> The world was all before them where to choose
> Their place of rest, and Providence their guide:
> They hand in hand with wandering steps and slow,
> Through Eden took their solitary way.

Bernard J. Paris

Optimism and Pessimism in *The Marble Faun*

There is little question that *The Marble Faun* includes Hawthorne's treatment of the concept of the fortunate fall; the fable
of the novel as well as explicit statements by the characters and
by the author bear witness to this. There has been some debate,
however, as to Hawthorne's attitude towards this concept. He
endorses it; the fall, as embodied in Donatello's sin, serves to raise
man above the state from which he fell, and hence good comes
out of evil.[1] He rejects it; "sin may be forgiven by God; softened
by penitence; still its stains persist; and its permanent effect is
not educative but warping."[2] A third point of view is represented
by Richard H. Fogle, who contends that "Hawthorne neither ac-
cepts nor rejects it. . . . He leaves the question in suspension, which
in *The Marble Faun* becomes the central mystery of man."[3] It
is possible to consider Hawthorne's attitude towards the concept
of *felix culpa* from yet another point of view; namely, that he
sees the fall as fortunate in some respects and as unfortunate in
others (it is a real fall, grounded in evil and involving the loss of a
good), and that he incorporates both of these perspectives into his
over-all vision. Hawthorne does not "[leave] the question in

Reprinted from *Boston University Studies in English,* II (1956), 95–112, by
permission of *Studies in Romanticism* (current copyright holder) and the
author.

[1] See Donald A. Ringe, "Hawthorne's Psychology of the Head and Heart,"
PMLA, LXV (1950), 120–132.
[2] Austin Warren, *Nathaniel Hawthorne,* American Writers Series (New
York: American Book Company, 1934), p. xxviii. See also, F. O. Matthiessen,
American Renaissance (New York: Oxford University Press, 1941), p. 310,
and, for the most recent discussion of the question, Hyatt H. Waggoner,
Hawthorne (Cambridge, Mass.: The Belknap Press of Harvard University
Press, 1945), pp. 195–222. Two articles which are relevant to my discussion
of *The Marble Faun* appeared while this essay was in proof; they are Merle
E. Brown, "The Structure of *The Marble Faun,*" *American Literature,*
XXVIII (1956), 302–313, and Henry G. Fairbanks, "Sin, Free Will, and
'Pessimism' in Hawthorne," *PMLA,* LXXI (1956), 975–989. Although I find
much to agree with (and much to disagree with) in these articles, neither, I
feel, has rendered my examination of the novel unnecessary, and neither
has induced me to alter my interpretation.
[3] *Hawthorne's Fiction: the Light and the Dark* (Norman: University of
Oklahoma Press, 1952), p. 163.

suspension" (is the fall essentially fortunate or unfortunate?); rather he makes a positive assertion: the fall is *both* fortunate *and* unfortunate. It is essential to recognize that Hawthorne is not treating the concept of *felix culpa* theologically, with all its Christological ramifications; he is reworking it, in secular terms, out of the fabric of contemporary life by examining the operation of the paradox in human history, life, and culture. We must be prepared, then, to base our conclusions about Hawthorne's attitude towards the concept upon an examination of the particularities of his treatment of it.

It would be a mistake, however, considering that what we are above all trying to achieve is an understanding of *The Marble Faun* as an autonomous work of art, to orient our consideration of the novel completely around the question of Hawthorne's attitude towards the concept of the fortunate fall. An interpretive discussion of a work of art should in some sense mirror the structure and the distributions of emphasis present in the work itself. The starting point for an analysis of *The Marble Faun* that has as its aim a perception of the statement that the novel makes about life is, it seems to me, an examination of the fable.[4] The keynote of the fable of the novel is the initial conception of placing, or misplacing, the innocent, simple, Arcadian Donatello in the context of the sophisticated and sin-burdened life of nineteenth-century civilization. A large part of the novel's significance certainly lies in observing what happens (necessarily, I think Hawthorne would insist) as a result of this mismating of man and environment, especially when we consider the nature of the man and of the environment in question. What happens is that the innocent Donatello sins and as a consequence becomes very much like the rest of mankind. The fable of the novel has often been characterized as Hawthorne's reworking of the fall of man. In addition to this, and *in combination with it*, the fable presents the moral, spiritual, and intellectual development that a man undergoes in his growth from childhood to maturity. To put this in its largest terms, the novel takes as its subject the evolution of the human race from its most primitive state, in which it is hardly separated from the lower animals, to its most civilized state, in which, unfortunately, there is a higher refinement of evil as well as of intellect.

---

[4] Darrel Abel, in "A Masque of Love and Death," *University of Toronto Quarterly*, XXIII (1953), 9–25, an extremely interesting article which came to my attention after this essay was written, discusses *The Marble Faun* very fruitfully in terms of "the symbolism of characters."

Donatello, although he is the fully developed product of an Arcadian civilization, is a child in terms of his nineteenth-century environment. Miriam, Kenyon, and Hilda are cognizant of this:

> In social intercourse, these familiar friends of his habitually and instinctively allowed for him, as for a child or some other lawless thing, exacting no strict obedience to conventional rules, and hardly noticing his eccentricities enough to pardon them. There was an indefinable characteristic about Donatello that set him outside of rules. (Chapter ɪɪ)

It is a sign of Donatello's later maturity that he feels compelled to submit himself to punishment by civil authorities. Miriam continually speaks of Donatello as a child. His resemblance to the marble faun associates him with the childhood of the race. Miriam says:

> "Imagine, now, a real being, similar to this mythic Faun; how happy, how genial, how satisfactory would be his life, enjoying the warm, sensuous, earthy side of nature; revelling in the merriment of woods and streams; living as our four-footed kindred do,—as mankind did in its innocent childhood." (Chapter ɪɪ)

Mankind, of course, is no longer in its innocent childhood, and Donatello cannot lead the life for which his nature was formed. He does, however, get a taste of this life in rare moments of escape from his unhappy plight. He fully reassumes his faun-like attributes in the natural surroundings of the Borghese Gardens, and "his joy was like that of a child that had gone astray from home, and finds himself suddenly in his mother's arms again" (Chapter VIII). Donatello's communion with nature is presented as an aspect of childhood. After the murder, when Donatello attempts to renew his contact with the wild creatures in the woods of Monte Beni, he tells Kenyon, " 'I doubt . . . whether they will remember my voice now. It changes, you know, as the boy grows towards manhood.' " When his fears are realized, Kenyon consoles him by saying, " 'We all of us, as we grow older . . . lose somewhat of our proximity to nature. It is the price we pay for experience' " (Chapter XXVII).

Donatello as we first meet him, then, is an anomaly in his environment. He is a child who, in the course of the novel, becomes a man. But the unhappy fact is that he must sin to become a man, as men are constituted in modern civilization, where sinfulness, or the suffering connected with it, is part of one's heritage and, consequently, an integral part of manhood, of maturity, itself. Even before the murder Donatello is undergoing a gradual change as his environment impinges upon his essential nature. Miriam tells Donatello: " 'You are getting spoilt in this dreary Rome, and will be as wise and as wretched as all the rest of mankind, unless you go back to your Tuscan vineyards' " (Chapter XVI). And in the opening chapter Hilda comments on Donatello's resemblance to the Faun of Praxiteles: " 'If there is any difference between the two faces, the reason may be, I suppose, that the Faun dwelt in woods and fields, and consorted with his like; whereas Donatello has known cities a little, and such people as ourselves.' " His initial identification with the marble Faun of Praxiteles enables the marble statue to serve as a fixed pole by which we can estimate the degree of change in Donatello. As Hilda's comment shows, Donatello has already begun to change, and the course of his development is initially away from the Faun, and then back towards the Faun, but with a difference. This circularity of movement is a recurrent pattern in the novel and, as will be shown later, it corresponds both to the over-all action and to a major aspect of the theme.

Granting the dislocation of the simple and innocent Donatello in his complex and guilt-burdened environment, the question arises, why must Donatello sin? Hilda, after all, remains innocent (though she does not fully escape the consequences of sin). The novel presents us with two kinds of innocence: the subhuman innocence of Donatello (to use R. H. Fogle's terms) and the superhuman innocence of Hilda. Hilda's innocence suffers no more change than to be somewhat sophisticated by the knowledge that evil exists in the world. Her saint-like nature, however, is impervious to the harmful effects of her evil environment; her moral character remains essentially the same. Hilda, despite her spirituality, is a product of civilization, and as such she can find a home in it, even if this home is attained through spiritual, moral, and physical isolation. She has, in a sense, risen out of her environment; Donatello has yet to be a part of it. He is cast into a completely foreign cultural complex, one that clashes violently with his hereditary nature, and consequently he is highly susceptible to external influences.

But this is not the entire reason why Donatello must sin. He must sin in order to survive. The nineteenth century taught that an organism must be in harmony with its environment; if it is not, it must adapt itself or perish. This is precisely Donatello's situation. We recall that Donatello is the sole survivor of a once numerous family, a family which is apparently doomed to extinction. Commenting on this, Thomaso, Donatello's butler, tells Kenyon, " 'The world has grown either too evil, or else too wise and sad, for such men as the old Counts of Monte Beni used to be' " (Chapter XXVI). In discussing the long, unbroken history of the Monte Beni family, Hawthorne writes:

> The successive members of the Monte Beni family showed valor and policy enough, at all events, to keep their herditary possessions out of the clutch of grasping neighbors, and probably differed very little from the other feudal barons with whom they fought and feasted. Such a degree of conformity with the manners of the generations, through which it survived, must have been essential to the prolonged continuance of the race. (Chapter xxvi)

But Donatello, it is stressed, is not an ordinary Count of Monte Beni; he is one of the periodically recurring sons who exactly resemble the original Faun from whose union with a mortal woman the Monte Beni family derived. He is not, therefore, possessed of those attributes which allowed most of his forebears to adapt themselves to the civilization of the day and thus insure "the prolonged continuance of the race." In addition, as Tomaso's remark indicates, the environment has become increasingly inimical to the Monte Beni nature. Donatello is a complete anomaly in his environment and must adapt or perish. In the final chapter of the novel Kenyon remarks to Hilda:

> "It seems the moral of his story, that human beings of Donatello's character, compounded especially for happiness, have no longer any business on earth. . . . Life has grown so sadly serious, that such men must change their nature, or else perish, like the antediluvian creatures, that required as the condition of their existence, a more summer-like atmosphere than ours."

This quotation reveals a line of thought that continually complements the concept of the fortunate fall. In Chapter V, Miriam had told Donatello: " 'You are a Faun, you know. . . . But the world is sadly changed nowadays; grievously changed, poor Donatello. . . . You have appeared on earth some centuries too late.' " There is a decided strain of primitivism in *The Marble Faun*. Donatello's original faun-like nature and the life he would have led in the Golden Age are presented very attractively. Man, in his development from the childhood of the race, has lost his gaiety and innocence, and his ability to commune with nature. The world has "grievously changed." This sense of loss is most completely expressed in one of Kenyon's introspections:

> Mankind are getting so far beyond the childhood of their race that they scorn to be happy any longer. A simple and joyous character can find no place for itself among the sage and sombre figures that would put his unsophisticated cheerfulness to shame. The entire system of man's affairs, as at present established, is built up purposely to exclude the careless and happy soul. . . . Therefore it was—so, at least, the sculptor thought, . . . —that the young Count found it impossible nowadays to be what his forefathers had been. . . . Nature, in beast, fowl, and tree, and earth, flood, and sky, is what it was of old; but sin, care, and self-consciousness have set the human portion of the world askew; and thus the simplest character is ever the soonest to go astray. (Chapter XXVI)

This indictment of contemporary civilization represents Hawthorne's pessimistic point of view, in contrast to the optimism embodied in the concept of the fortunate fall. It is a statement of the common primitivistic position that as society moves farther away from the simplicity of the Golden Age and Arcadian times it becomes progressively more somber and corrupt. (This is not to say that Hawthorne prescribes any mode of conduct other than one based on an acceptance of our post-lapsarian state. It is a sin not to accept the limitations imposed upon us by the fact of our existence in an imperfect and sinful world. But, in *The Marble Faun*, Hawthorne's position is that, although we must accept the corrupted state of contemporary life and make the best of it, for good can come of evil, this is not the only conceivable mode of human existence; this is not the best of all possible worlds.) The full implication of this pessimism is manifested when we realize that an innocent creature like Donatello must sin in order to survive.

This pessimism, however, does not represent Hawthorne's final position. As we shall see, modern civilization and even sin and suffering have many important advantages over Arcadian innocence and simplicity. Further, and more pertinent at the moment, Arcadian creatures and civilization have, even in their own terms, some unsavory characteristics. To cite but one example, in his account of those Counts of Monte Beni that reproduce the attributes of their Faun forefather, Hawthorne, after describing the attractive aspects of their nature, continues:

> On the other hand, there were deficiencies both of intellect and heart, and especially, as it seemed, in the development of the higher portion of man's nature. These defects were less perceptible in early youth, but showed themselves more strongly with advancing age, when, as the animal spirits settled down upon a lower level, the representative of the Monte Benis was apt to become sensual, addicted to gross pleasures, heavy, unsympathizing, and insulated within the narrow limits of a surly selfishness. (Chapter xxxvi)

II

We come now to the centrally important matter of Hawthorne's ambi-focal or multi-focal perspective. As has been demonstrated, a strong case can be made for Hawthorne's pessimism, although the primitivism from which this pessimism derives is not without qualification. The qualification of the pessimistic point of view leads to a kind of optimism. If the Golden Age had its serious drawbacks, then the development of the race from its childhood brings with it certain advantages. The chief embodiment of the optimistic point of view is in the concept of the fortunate fall, and many good arguments can and will be advanced to indicate Hawthorne's endorsement of this position. But Hawthorne's optimism also has intrinsic qualifications, and, of course, it is strongly counterbalanced by primitivism and its resultant pessimism. The crux is not that Hawthorne asserts and then denies each point of view, but that his vision is broad enough to include them all simultaneously. Truth is not simple, but complex. The optimistic and the pessimistic points of view, which qualify each other, and their respective intrinsic qualifications, are all valid.

This multi-focal perspective is operative not only with regard to the central fable, but also in Hawthorne's presentation of most of the subordinate elements in the novel. It is evidenced, for example, in Hawthorne's treatment of Rome, of the Catholic Church, of the past, and of the major characters.[5] Perhaps the best way to clarify

---

[5] For an interesting discussion of Hawthorne's attitude of mingled attraction and repulsion towards Rome and the past see Christof Wegelin, "Europe in Hawthorne's Fiction," *ELH,* XIV (1947), 219–245. Wegelin states (p. 219) that Hawthorne, "linking the question of the Old World firmly with the

the nature of this perspective is to illustrate it by a detailed examination of its operation in several specific instances. There is no
question that Miriam and Donatello sin in murdering the model,
but is this a totally evil act? It affects Miriam and Donatello as if
it were, but this makes it evil in a psychological rather than an
absolute sense. The model is, after all, depraved, a bane to the
world. The murder takes place at the Tarpeian Rock, and just before the model's appearance Miriam tells Donatello that the Roman
custom of flinging criminals from the rock was justified, for those
who thus met their doom were

> "men that cumbered the world. . . . Men whose lives were the bane
> of their fellow-creatures. Men who poisoned the air, which is the
> common breath of all, for their own selfish purposes. . . . It was
> well done . . .; innocent persons were saved by the destruction of
> a guilty one, who deserved his doom." (Chapter xvɪɪɪ)

Immediately after the murder Miriam tells Donatello: " 'Surely, it
is no crime that we have committed. One wretched and worthless
life ·has been sacrificed to cement two other lives for evermore' "
(Chapter XIX). Later the murder is symbolically repeated in a
way that leads us to question its evilness. While they are atop the
tower at Monte Beni, Kenyon and Donatello discuss a delicate
plant which has grown from the crumbling mortar in the crevices
of the roof. (The plant symbolizes Miriam, who derived from a
decadent family in an atmosphere of sin.) Kenyon tells Donatello
to seek for the moral embodied in the shrub's existence. " 'It
teaches me nothing,' said the simple Donatello, stooping over the
plant, and perplexing himself with a minute scrutiny. 'But here
was a worm that would have killed it; an ugly creature, which I
will fling over the battlements . . .' " (Chapter XXVIII). This
double perspective is urged by Kenyon in a conversation with
Hilda. Kenyon maintains that there may be a " 'mixture of good
. . . in things evil' " and that when all the circumstances surrounding Miriam's and Donatello's deed are considered " 'I know not
well how to distinguish it from much that the world calls heroism.
Might we not render some such verdict as this?—Worthy of Death,
but not unworthy of Love!' "

problem of morals . . . turned to a careful comparison of values—to weighing
the moral burden against the aesthetic wealth both of which resulted from
the European past."

"Never!" answered Hilda.... "There is, I believe, only one right and one wrong; and I do not understand . . . how two things so totally unlike can be mistaken for one another; nor how two mortal foes, as Right and Wrong surely are, can work together in the same deed. This is my faith; and I should be led astray, if you could persuade me to give it up."

"Alas for poor human nature, then!" said Kenyon, sadly, and yet half smiling at Hilda's unworldly and impractical theory. (Chapter XLII)

We find, then, co-present in the novel, both the ambi-focal perspective—presented here by Kenyon—that pervades the whole, and, embodied in Hilda, its opposite, a uni-focal perspective. It is apparent which Hawthorne deems valid.

Hawthorne's presentation of Hilda also has a double nature. Our judgment of Hilda depends upon whether we view her in terms of human or divine values. The whole texture of the novel tends to reject Hilda's uncompromising, uni-focal view of the relation between good and evil in favor of an ambi-focal perspective. Yet when we consider Hilda as essentially a spiritual being we feel that this point of view is proper for her, even if for no one else. Both Kenyon and Miriam recognize her rejection of Miriam after the murder as in keeping with the spirituality of her nature and as necessary for the maintenance of her whiteness and purity. Hilda's spirituality itself, however, is not unequivocally accepted as a good. It too is seen in terms of both the human and the divine, as is indicated by the following passage. Miriam is ascending the staircase of Hilda's tower.

Miriam passed beneath the deep portal of the palace, and turning to the left, began to mount flight after flight of a staircase, which, for the loftiness of its aspiration, was worthy to be Jacob's ladder, or, at all events, the staircase of the Tower of Babel. (Chapter VI)

Judged by earthly standards Hilda is found to be in danger of spiritual pride and wanting in human sympathy. The fact that she maintains a uni-focal point of view automatically acts as a criticism; it is the essence of what is wrong with Hilda insofar as it governs her actions towards her fellow beings.

In the final chapter, as we shall see, the ambi-focal and the uni-focal points of view are shown in direct conflict, as Kenyon draws the moral of Donatello's story in terms of both optimism and pessi-

mism and finds himself opposed by Hilda. Kenyon's capitulation
does not mark the defeat of the ambi-focal by the uni-focal perspective, but rather the triumph of human over purely intellectual
values.

In this connection, let us consider the sub-plot of the novel, the
Hilda-Kenyon story, in itself and in its relation to the whole. As
the main plot may be seen as the maturation and humanization of
Donatello, so the sub-plot, which gains its impetus from the main
plot, may be seen as the maturation, in a somewhat different sense,
and humanization of Hilda. In both cases, the instrument through
which the development takes place is Miriam, the representative
of nineteenth-century European civilization. In each case the development culminates in a mature love relationship (Miriam and
Donatello, Kenyon and Hilda) that would otherwise have been
impossible. Hilda and Donatello each move from isolation to inte-
gration in the human family; the human triumphs over the subhuman and the superhuman. This process is, in both cases, presented as inevitable. Kenyon, the man of marble, under the impetus
of his love for Hilda, comes to give the human precedence over the
non-human. When Kenyon comes to meet Miriam and Donatello
on the Campagna, hoping to gain news of the missing Hilda, he
finds a magnificent statue which has just been unearthed. He
should be elated. "He could hardly, we fear, be reckoned a consummate artist, because there was something dearer to him than
his art; and, by the greater strength of a human affection, the
divine statue seemed to fall asunder again, and become only a heap
of worthless fragments" (Chapter XLVI). It is for the same reason
(and this has usually not been understood) that Kenyon, in the
final chapter, forsakes his ambi-focal point of view under the pressure of Hilda's objections, crying " 'I never did believe it!' " and
" 'O Hilda, guide me home!' " Hilda's love is, rightly, more important to Kenyon than any intellectual conception, even if that
conception is a valid and profound one.

Hilda's initial relation to Roman civilization is similar to Donatello's; they are both outside it, though both are linked to it
through Miriam. Donatello, because he is in a state of development
beneath that of his environment, must sin to identify himself with
it and survive in it. Identification is not necessary to survival for
Hilda, but it is nevertheless inevitable because of the inter-con-
nectedness of human beings. As a result of her despair at the discovery of evil in the world Hilda loses her ability to be a perfect
copyist of the old masters. She goes through a completely negative
period, corresponding to Donatello's at Monte Beni, in which the

greatest art seems valueless; her ability to perceive the truth of human falseness is so heightened that everything, even truth, seems like deceit. Hilda never fully regains her powers as a copyist, but after her confession she reaches a state of synthesis that is parallel (as we shall see) to Donatello's state of mingled human and faun. "On her part, Hilda returned to her customary occupations with a fresh love for them, and yet a deeper look into the heart of things; such as those necessarily acquire who have passed from picture galleries into dungeon gloom, and thence come back to the picture gallery again" (Chapter XLI).

Hilda had been accustomed to look at life from the divine, uni-focal, point of view. Here is how Hawthorne describes her original paintings: "scenes delicately imagined, lacking, perhaps, the reality which comes only from a close acquaintance with life, but so softly touched with feeling and fancy, that you seemed to be looking at humanity with angel's eyes. With years and experience she might be expected to attain a darker and more forcible touch, which would impart to her designs the relief they needed" (Chapter VI). Hilda's humanization does not lead her to give up her uni-focal point of view. Here again there is a synthesis: she retains her point of view, but her actions toward her fellows are motivated less by judgment than by the love and human sympathy she has gained from her experience. Hilda had little understanding of the need that human beings have of each other because she had always been self-sufficient in her spirituality. She had little awareness of her human limitations and hence of the limitations of others. She finds, however, that her purity and spirituality, her religious devotion, are unable to cope with, or help her in, the suffering caused by her knowledge of Miriam's crime. She finds herself, for the first time, in need of human aid. In the absence of Kenyon (who has been offering Donatello a human solution to his problems and turning him from thoughts of a monastic life [6]), Hilda finds human succor in the form of the Catholic confessional. In keeping with Hawthorne's ambi-focal point of view, it is the humanness of the Catholic Church that is at once its glory and its shame.

III

Keeping in mind the pessimistic point of view that derived from Hawthorne's tendency towards primitivism (which constitutes his affirmation of the fall), and the ambi-focal nature of his over-all perspective, let us now consider the manner in which the concept

---

[6] See Chapter XXIX, and p. 76 below.

of the fortunate fall is embodied in the fable of *The Marble Faun*. The novel as a whole charts the course of Donatello's maturation and adaptation to his sin-laden surroundings.

The past plays a significant role in this development. The immediate agent in Donatello's evolution from a child-like and innocent primitive to an intellectually and spiritually developed, but guilt-burdened, man is his love for Miriam. Miriam is a distinctively European product.[7] Indeed, she may be considered the European counterpart of Hilda; for Miriam, it must be remembered, was innocent of any guilty action before the murder.[8] The shadow which hangs over her in the form of the model is the result of her European origin. Although the nature of the crime that haunts the innocent Miriam's footsteps is never made quite clear, it evidently stemmed from her refusal to marry the depraved kinsman to whom she had been pledged. The components of this situation, forced marriage and marriage to a kinsman, are evident attributes of a decadent civilization. Further, the depravity of the kinsman is attributed to the same kind of inbreeding. His character "betrayed traits so evil, so treacherous, so vile, and yet so strangely subtle, as could only be accounted for by the insanity which often develops itself in old, close-kept races of men, when long unmixed with newer blood" (Chapter XLVII). In one sense, the difference between Miriam and Hilda is the difference between their European and American backgrounds. " 'You should go with me to my native country,' observed the sculptor to Donatello. 'In that fortunate land, each generation has only its own sins and sorrows to bear. Here, it seems as if all the weary and dreary Past were piled upon the back of the Present' " (Chapter XXXIII).

---

[7] See Marius Bewley, *The Complex Fate* (London: Chatto and Windus, 1952), p. 49.

[8] Scholars are not agreed on the question of Miriam's innocence before the murder of the model. For an account of the scholarly disagreement, see Edward Wagenknecht, *Cavalcade of the American Novel* (New York: Henry Holt, 1952), p. 49, n. 23. The novel provides conclusive evidence of Miriam's innocence, although in the early chapters Hawthorne purposely obscures the question. For example, when Miriam visits Kenyon's studio for the purpose of unburdening herself to him, she says, "my conscience is still as white as Hilda's" (Chapter XIV). In Chapter XLVII, when Kenyon meets Miriam and Donatello on the Campagna, Miriam tells him about her past and reveals her true identity. " 'You shudder at me, I perceive,' said Miriam, suddenly interrupting her narrative. 'No; you were innocent,' replied the sculptor. 'I shudder at the fatality that seems to haunt your footsteps, and throws a shadow of crime about your path, you being guiltless.' 'There was such a fatality,' said Miriam; 'yes; the shadow fell upon me, innocent, but I went astray in it, and wandered—as Hilda could tell you—into crime.' "

Miriam's model, the Spectre of the Catacomb, whatever else he might symbolize,[9] represents her past, which was sin-darkened though not guilt-stained. Miriam comes to Rome to escape her past, but her effort is futile. The power that the model holds over Miriam is the threat that he will reveal to her friends the crime of which she has been accused. His appearance in the catacomb of St. Calixtus and the connection made in the popular mind between the model and the story of Memmius give him an additional association with the sinful past. The model, of course, stands for everything that is repugnant to Donatello, for everything in his environment that oppresses him. In opposition to the time-laden quality of the model, of Miriam, and of Rome, Donatello, in his undeveloped state, has no sense of time whatever; he has no idea even of his own age. When Donatello, in the Borghese Gardens, momentarily draws Miriam back into the Golden Age, she asks, " 'But, Donatello, how long will this happiness last?' " " 'How long!' he exclaimed; for it perplexed him even more to think of the future than to remember the past. 'Why should it have any end? How long! Forever! forever! forever!' " (Chapter IX). It is indicative of the vast change which Donatello had undergone in the course of the novel that he replies to Miriam's plea to prolong the days of their happiness on the Campagna by saying, " 'I dare not linger upon it. . . . I dare to be so happy as you have seen me, only because I have felt the time to be so brief' " (Chapter XLVII).

It is inevitable that Miriam, the product of a decadent civilization, will bring Donatello into contact with guilt and suffering. Miriam herself strongly warns Donatello of this several times, but Donatello is determined to follow her. He says, in the catacomb, " 'I will seek her, be the darkness ever so dismal . . .' " (Chapter IV). And later he tells Miriam, " 'Shroud yourself in what gloom you will, I must needs follow you' " (Chapter V). The question arises as to the nature of the attraction that links Donatello to Miriam. The following passage provides an answer:

> It might have been imagined that Donatello's unsophisticated heart would be more readily attracted to a feminine nature of clear simplicity like his own, than to one already turbid with grief

[9] See Dorothy Waples, "Suggestions for Interpreting *The Marble Faun,*" *American Literature,* XIII (1941), 224–239. The fable of the novel is seen as "the struggle between the death instinct represented by the spectre and the life instinct represented by Donatello." See also the article by Darrel Abel cited in n. 4.

or wrong, as Miriam's seemed to be. Perhaps, on the other hand,
his character needed the dark element, which it found in her.
(Chapter IX)

It is of man's nature and destiny to mature. Donatello's plight and
his process of maturation are presented in terms of light imagery.
Donatello is initially associated with pure sunshine, which belongs
to man's childhood, when sorrow and guilt have not yet made their
appearance. In his modern environment Donatello suffers because
he is endowed with an excess of light. Miriam, on the other hand,
presents an aspect of mingled light and shade, corresponding to the
mixture of good and evil in modern civilization. This is the state
at which Donatello must arrive if he is to survive. We recall Donatello's initial hatred of darkness and gloom. In the catacomb he
exclaims, " 'I hate it all! . . . Dear friends, let us hasten back into
the blessed daylight' " (Chapter III). The Roman environment
and, especially, his contact with the model throw a shadow upon
his nature. With the murder he is plunged into complete darkness.
Kenyon is surprised to find Donatello taking up his residence in
the gloomy tower and keeping all-night vigils with owls for his
companions. We also note Donatello's indifference to the Sunshine
wine of Monte Beni, which is symbolic of his original nature. The
summer at Monte Beni is the low point of Donatello's development.
He becomes moody and introspective, thinking only of his guilt and
contemplating the death's-head left to the family by an earlier
faun-like Count of Monte Beni who was also stained with blood
guilt. Kenyon, however, sees signs of intellectual and spiritual
maturation in Donatello, which he feels can ultimately have a good
result. He is aware that Donatello is burdened with a secret sorrow
and to him

> the effect of this hard lesson upon Donatello's intellect and dispo-
> sition was very striking. It was perceptible that he had already had
> glimpses of strange and subtle matters in those dark caverns,
> into which all men must descend, if they would know anything
> beneath the surface and illusive pleasures of existence. And when
> they emerge, though dazzled and blinded by the first glare of
> daylight, they take truer and sadder views of life forever after-
> wards. (Chapter XXIX)

The pattern of light imagery in this passage characterizes the nature of Donatello's development. He moves from pure light to

complete darkness, and he emerges wiser and more perceptive with a tempered light, a mingled light and shadow.

Viewed in terms of the thesis-antithesis-synthesis (a synthesis involving a transcendence) pattern apparent here, Donatello's development embodies the concept of the fortunate fall. The mingled light and shade of civilization affords man a sadder but truer view of life than the undiluted sunshine of the Golden Age. Further, it enables one to experience deeper and intenser pleasures than Donatello's initial faun-like gaiety. Hawthorne says of Donatello's and Miriam's sportiveness in the Borghese Gardens: "It was a glimpse far backward into Arcadian life, or, further still, into the Golden Age, before mankind was burdened with sin and sorrow, and before pleasure had been darkened with those shadows that bring it into high relief and make it happiness" (Chapter IX). We find this conception stated explicitly in terms of Adam's fall. Hawthorne writes of the summer at Monte Beni:

> It is possible, indeed, that even Donatello's grief and Kenyon's pale, sunless affection lent a charm to Monte Beni, which it would not have retained amid a more abundant joyousness. The sculptor strayed amid its vineyards and orchards, its dells and tangled shrubberies, with somewhat the sensations of an adventurer who should find his way to the site of ancient Eden, and behold its loveliness through the transparency of that gloom which has been brooding over those haunts of innocence ever since the fall. Adam saw it in a brighter sunshine, but never knew the shade of pensive beauty which Eden won from his expulsion. (Chapter xxx)

We find, then, that Hawthorne's optimism, deriving from the concept of the fortunate fall, is just as strongly presented as his pessimism, which stems from primitivism. But just as the pessimistic point of view had intrinsic qualifications which led in the direction of optimism, so the optimistic point of view has intrinsic qualifications which tend towards pessimism. Donatello, as we see him on the Campagna, has reached a state of ideal blending of light and shade that would enable him to experience the best of both worlds, Arcadian and modern. This mingled state represents, if Hawthorne ever expresses it, an absolute good, but the only way Donatello could achieve it was through sin. Kenyon has misgivings about the permanence of Miriam's and Donatello's bliss; today they are perfectly adjusted, "tomorrow,—a remorseful man and woman linked by a marriage-bond of crime,—they would set forth towards an inevitable goal" (Chapter XLVII). While Donatello's sin ultimately enables him to enjoy the advantages of a civilized state, it also obliges him to partake of its evils. He feels that he must suffer the punishment assigned by civil authorities for his crime. Miriam realizes the serious limitations of the civil government of Rome: she tells Kenyon, " 'I have assured him that there is no such thing as earthly justice, and especially none here, under the head of Christendom' " (Chapter XLVII). Thus the optimism arising from the perception of the thesis-antithesis-synthesis pattern outlined above is qualified by a recognition of the corruption of civilized society—a society to which Donatello's maturation forces him to commit himself. After Kenyon has encountered Donatello dressed as a penitent, Hawthorne remarks: "The growth of a soul . . . seemed hardly worth the heavy price that it had cost, in the sacrifice of those simple enjoyments that were gone forever. A creature of antique healthfulness had vanished from the earth; and, in his stead, there was only one other morbid and remorseful man, among millions that were cast in the same indistinguishable mould" (Chapter XLIII).

The pattern present in certain aspects of Hawthorne's light imagery is re-enforced by another aspect of the novel. As has been mentioned, the statue of the marble Faun serves as a pole by which we can chart the course of Donatello's development by observing his similarity to and divergence from it. Initially the resemblance is complete. Donatello's contact with the Roman environment and with the model causes a lessening of the resemblance. After the murder the similarity between Donatello and the statue is practically non-existent. Gradually, however, as Donatello's understanding deepens and he is led by Kenyon to new spiritual insights, the resemblance begins to reassert itself. When Donatello, in his spiritual isolation and brooding introspection, tells Kenyon that he is thinking of becoming a monk, Kenyon dissuades him and suggests, instead, a life of service to his fellow men.

> His face brightened beneath the stars; and, looking at it through the twilight, the sculptor's remembrance went back to that scene in the Capitol, where, both in features and expression, Donatello had seemed identical with the Faun. And still there was a resemblance; for now, when first the idea was suggested of living for the welfare of his fellow creatures, the original beauty, which sorrow had partly effaced, came back elevated and spiritualized. In the black depths, the Faun had found a soul, and was struggling with it towards the light of heaven. (Chapter XXIX)

Under the impetus of a growing desire for spiritual communion with his fellows which gradually lightens his initially crushing burden of guilt and leads him to relinquish his self-destructive efforts at repentance, Donatello reassumes more and more of his original nature. The elements of his original faun-like nature and his newly acquired seriousness, intelligence, and insight are mingled, just as his original sunshine and his subsequent darkness and gloom are mingled.

Donatello's development has been, in a defined sense, circular; he has returned to the point from which he started, but considerably altered. The pattern of the novel as a whole is circular; it begins in spring and ends in spring. The pattern is one of birth, death, and rebirth to a higher kind of existence. Miriam comments on this circularity in Donatello's development and she proceeds to draw an appropriate moral.

"Is he not beautiful? . . . So changed, yet still, in a deeper sense, so much the same! He has travelled in a circle, as all things heavenly and earthly do, and now comes back to his original self, with an inestimable treasure of improvement won from an experience of pain. . . . Was the crime—in which he and I were wedded— was it a blessing, in that strange disguise? Was it a means of education, bringing a simple and imperfect nature to a point of feeling and intelligence which it could have reached under no other discipline?" (Chapter XLVII)

Miriam now proposes, in explicit terms, the doctrine of the fortunate fall.

It is neither wise nor possible to ignore Kenyon's summation of the meaning of the action of the novel in the last chapter. What Kenyon says before his capitulation to Hilda represents, it seems to me, Hawthorne's final position. Hilda's objections are quite in keeping with her character and her uni-focal point of view, but they are not at all consonant with anything else in the novel. Kenyon first offers as the moral of the story the pessimistic point of view. When Hilda rejects this, he tells her, " 'Then here is another; take your choice,' " and he proceeds to expound the optimistic concept of the fortunate fall. The implication is clear: both of these positions are valid. Here, in part, is the passage.

"It seems the moral of his story, that human beings of Donatello's character, compounded especially for happiness, have no longer any business on earth, or elsewhere. Life has grown so sadly serious, that such men must change their nature, or else perish, like the antediluvian creatures, that required as the condition of their existence, a more summer-like atmosphere than ours."

"I will not accept your moral!" replied the hopeful and happy-natured Hilda.

"Then here is another; take your choice!" said the sculptor. . . . "Sin has educated Donatello, and elevated him. Is sin, then,—which we deem such a dreadful blackness in the universe,—is it, like sorrow, merely an element of human education, through which we struggle to a higher and purer state than we could otherwise have attained? Did Adam fall, that we might ultimately rise to a far loftier paradise than his?"

Each of these positions is valid, but, taken separately, represents only a partial view. Taken together, they embody a complete and complex view of a profound problem of human existence. Modern civilization is to be considered an intricate blending of good and bad; it is to be viewed with a subtle mingling of optimism and pessimism.

Thus, in utilizing the concept of the fortunate fall in *The Marble Faun,* Hawthorne has searched for all its inherent connotations; he has redefined it for himself by separating it out into its component elements. Man's development from simplicity to complexity has enabled him to experience depths of emotion of which Adam was incapable; it has enabled him to create and perceive beauty all the richer for an element of shadow that has its origin in guilt and suffering; it has enabled him to penetrate "beneath the surface and illusive pleasures of existence." But, at the same time, this development has been from innocence to guilt, from joyousness to sadness, from naturalness to sophistication and artificiality, from communion with nature to separation and isolation. *The Marble Faun* is not a dialectical treatment of a subtle question of theology; it is a representation of the nature of human existence as Hawthorne perceives it. Hawthorne is obliged to affirm no theory; he merely pictures. His picture, of course, constitutes an affirmation; but, by virtue of being a picture and not an argument, it can affirm all that comes within its compass. Hawthorne fully insists upon the paradoxical nature of the concept of the fortunate fall which often tends to become blunted by a disproportionate emphasis on one of its two terms. In a word, he affirms not merely a *fall,* nor simply a *fortunate* fall, but a *fortunate fall.*

Sacvan Bercovitch

Of Wise and Foolish Virgins: Hilda *Versus* Miriam in Hawthorne's *Marble Faun*

Hawthorne's critics have often puzzled over Hilda's rejection of Miriam in *The Marble Faun*. The fair-haired New Englander appears to be almost a model of Christian virtue, yet in her best friend's crucial moment of need she denies her all help or even sympathy. When, soon after the Capuchin's murder, Miriam seeks her out, she withdraws "shuddering" in "terror" and exclaims in a mixed tone of "sorrowful entreaty" and self-righteous "confidence":

> Do not come nearer, Miriam! ... If I were one of God's angels, with a nature incapable of stain ... I would keep ever at your side and try to lead you upward. But I am a poor, lonely girl, whom God has set here in an evil world, and given her only a white robe, and bid her wear it back to Him, as white as when she put it on. ... And, therefore ... I mean ... henceforth to avoid you.[1]

Miriam bitterly denounces the lack of compassion in this response, and most modern readers have shared her reaction. In general, they have explained the scene as revealing a minor flaw or a momentary lapse in Hilda's moral stance.[2] But it seems unlikely that Hawthorne would have chosen this climactic episode, this central test of values, to introduce an uncharacteristic blemish in an otherwise saintly figure. Miriam herself suggests a more persuasive approach. Hilda's harshness, she observes, expresses a basic personality defect—" 'I always said, Hilda, that you were merciless; for I had a perception of it, even while you loved me best' " (p. 243)

Reprinted from *New England Quarterly,* XLI (June, 1968), 281–86, with the permission of the *New England Quarterly* and the author.
[1] *The Marble Faun,* in *The Works of Hawthorne,* edited by George Parsons Lathrop (Boston, 1891), VI, 240–241, 243; all references to the novel are from this edition.
[2] See, for example, Terence Martin, *Nathaniel Hawthorne* (New York, 1965), 173 ff. Hyatt H. Waggoner argues that the mote is only in our own (and Miriam's) eyes: the idea that Hilda is ever "uncharitable," he maintains, "would have shocked Hawthorne immeasurably." *Hawthorne, A Critical Study* (Cambridge, Mass., 1963), 221–222. But see footnote 3, below, and my note on "Hilda's 'Seven-Branched Allegory,' " *EALN,* I, 5–7 (1966).

—and several recent critics have attempted to expand her observation. Sheldon W. Leibman, for example, argues that Hilda's repudiation shows the overall "constriction or inhibition . . . [of her]
mind"; Richard H. Fogle sees in it an "inadequate" spiritual "simplicity" which "consistently rejects the complex" and which, therefore, "we cannot accept," here and elsewhere, as a proper
"judgment of earthly values." [3] Their view rightly emphasizes
Hawthorne's awareness of the young woman's limitations. Nonetheless, it overlooks, or oversimplifies, the nature of her "severity"
in this instance. The full meaning of the confrontation, I believe,
derives from the implicit analogy—sustained throughout the novel
—between Hilda and the "wise virgins" of Christ's Parable.

Perhaps the dominant image of Hilda pictures her as the cus-
todian of the Virgin's Shrine. Every aspect of her description sup-
ports the image: her white robe, the tower she lives in and the
doves she feeds, her vocation as copyist [4]—and, most directly, her
devoted tending of the eternal flame. She "religiously lit" and
"trimmed the lamp before the Virgin's shrine," writes Hawthorne
over and again, and kept "the flame of the never-dying lamp . . .
burning at noon, at *midnight*, and at all hours of the twenty-four"
(pp. 69, 374, 379; my italics). Professor Fogle finds in these passages an evocation of the vestal virgins, transformed in terms of
Christian worship.[5] More specifically, they seem to refer to the
faithful virgins in Matthew, who prepared their lamps with care,
so that when the "bridegroom" appeared "at midnight" they could
rise ready to "go . . . out to meet him." [6] Like them, Hilda guards
her virtue "in an evil world"; like them, she resolves to wear her
white robe "back to Him"; and like them, she turns away the sinner who seeks her aid. The parable, we recall, tells of ten virgins

> which took their lamps, and went forth to meet the bridegroom.
> And five of them were wise, and five *were* foolish. They that *were*
> foolish . . . took no oil with them: But the wise took oil in their
> vessels with the lamps. While the bridegroom tarried, they all . . .
> slept. And at midnight there was a cry made, Behold, the bride-

---

[3] Liebman, "The Design of *The Marble Faun*," *New England Quarterly*, XL,
67 (1967); Fogle, *Hawthorne's Fiction: The Light and the Dark* (Norman,
1952), 170–172.
[4] See Paul Brodtkorb, Jr., "Art Allegory in *The Marble Faun*," *PMLA*,
LXXVII, 254–267 (1962).
[5] *Hawthorne's Fiction*, 169.
[6] Mat. 25:6; King James Version.

groom cometh. . . . Then all those virgins arose. . . . And the foolish
said to the wise, Give us of your oil; for our lamps are gone out.
But the wise answered, saying, *Not so:* lest there be not enough for
us and you; but go ye rather to them that sell, and buy for your-
selves. (Mat. 5:1-9)

From this perspective, Hilda's action becomes at least morally intelligible. She recognizes her frailty and dares not jeopardize the
little grace granted to "a poor, lonely girl." A wise virgin, she decides to leave the dispensation to God. She refuses Miriam not out
of hardheartedness but in the conviction that she is impotent to
"save" her, that her foolish friend must find her own way "to them
that sell, and buy" for herself.

The foolish virgins' fate is, of course, made more explicit than
is Miriam's. "Christ," as Calvin notes, "mocking the knowledge
which they have acquired when it is too late, shows how their stu-
pidity will be punished": [7] after they have bought the oil, they return to find that "the door was shut" irrevocably upon them (Mat.
25: 10-12). This "mocking" irony was apparently too cruel—or in
any case, too final—for Hawthorne to adopt. It is true that he admits (through Kenyon) that the divine retribution for Miriam's
crime may show " 'cruelty . . . [and] not mercy' " (p. 526); [8] and,
more importantly, he makes her acknowledge the possibility of
damnation in terms which unmistakably echo the parable's conclusion. As Miriam and Donatello wander aimlessly from the precipice of their *midnight* crime (see p. 199),

it so chanced that they turned into a street, at one extremity of
which stood Hilda's tower. There was a light in her high chamber;
a light, too, at the Virgin's shrine. . . .
    "The good, pure, child! She is praying, Donatello," said Miriam.
. . . Then her own sin rushed upon her, and she shouted, with the
rich strength of her voice, "Pray for us, Hilda; we need it!"
    Whether Hilda heard and recognized the voice we cannot tell.
The window was immediately closed, and her form disappeared

---

[7] *Commentary On A Harmony of the Evangelists* . . . , tr. William Pringle
(Grand Rapids, Mich., 1949), III, 172.
[8] Regarding the pessimistic overtones of Hawthorne's view of Providence in
The Marble Faun, see Frederick C. Crews, *The Sins of the Fathers: Hawthorne's Psychological Themes* (New York, 1966), 214, 231–232, 236. The
earliest expression of this approach appears in Emile Montégut's 1860 review "Un Romancier Pessimiste en Amerique" in *Revue des Deux Mondes,*
which Walter Blair notes in *Eight American Authors: A Review of Research
and Criticism,* ed. Jay B. Hubbell (New York, 1963), 1914–15.

from behind the snowy curtain. Miriam felt this to be a token that
the cry of her condemned spirit was shut out of heaven. (pp. 208–
209)

Hilda's withdrawal behind the "snowy curtain" of her faith fore-
shadows her verbal rejection of Miriam, but the latter's interpretation of the gesture—that "her condemned spirit was [now] shut
out of heaven"—remains unresolved in the novel. Like his heroine,
Hawthorne leaves the problem of salvation to God.[9]

He does, however, offer a tentative affirmation of Hilda's choice.
From a theological standpoint, his outlook is most fully formulated
in the sermons of his Puritan forebears (who ameliorated the rigid
Calvinist dichotomy of elect and damned by stressing the sinner's
hope of attaining grace [10]) and, in particular, in Thomas Shepard's
lengthy discourse, *The Parable of the Ten Virgins Opened & Applied.* Shepard begins by posing the question usually raised by
contemporary readers in connection with Hilda's act: *"What then
are the wise unwilling to communicate of the Graces they have?
What Christian but is willing?"* [11] His immediate reply reflects
both the biblical text and Hilda's self-defense: the upright "know
all which they had in time of extremity was little enough for them
at this season." But he goes farther than this. Since, he contends,
"We have but our measure . . . it is not in our hands to dispense
grace in times of extremity, that must come from him [Christ]
that hath received the Spirit without measure." In this sense, the
denial of aid indicates not merely self-protection but, more largely,
a consideration of the others' best interest. It marks a deliberate
"check to their folly" who, neglecting God, "go to their fellow-
brethren for help, [crying:] our misery is great: oh now help us
with your grace." To these "misguided creatures" the wise render
"Counsel and advice directing them to the remedy. . . . *Go to them*

---

[9] In this regard, see the discussions of Hawthorne's ambiguous views of the
"fortunate fall" in Sidney P. Moss, "The Problem of Theme in *The Marble
Faun,*" *NCF,* XVIII, 399 (1964); and Edward Wagenknecht, *Nathaniel
Hawthorne: Man and Writer* (New York, 1961), 194–195.
[10] See Perry Miller, "Preparation for Salvation in Seventeenth-Century
New England," *JHI,* IV, 253–286 (1943); Calvin, of course, sees a proof of
the doctrine of the elect in the parable (*Commentary,* III, 173).
[11] *The Parable of the Ten Virgins Opened & Applied . . .* (London, 1660),
Part II, 89; cf. Calvin, *Commentary,* III, 172–173. Hawthorne's familiarity
with Puritan sermons is well known; Randall Stewart notes another connection between Thomas Shepard and certain ideas in *The Marble Faun*—
relating to Miriam's critique of Guido's Archangel—in *Nathaniel Hawthorne: A Biography* (New Haven, 1948), 245.

that sell and buy for your selves. [That is to say:] The Spirit of Grace comes not so lightly; You would have it given; no, you must buy it; you would have us help you; no, there are others appointed for to sell it you." In short, the denial stems both from humility and from true Christian compassion: the wise virgins "consider that God has now broken open the consciences of the foolish"; they understand, furthermore, that "other means are sanctified to beget Grace . . . or rather a greater efficacy and power; hence they send them to other means." [12]

It would be too much to say that Hilda—"daughter of the Puritans" though she is (pp. 71, 412, 454, 526)—reasons all this through when she sends Miriam from her studio. Yet surely she senses it on some half-conscious level. Though she never presumes to forgive, she prays that Miriam will receive pity and grace through "a greater efficacy and power"; though she reproves Kenyon for his *felix culpa* conjectures, her heart goes out (immediately afterwards) to the "kneeling figure" of Miriam—now a "female penitent" with "upturned face"—extending "her hands with a gesture of benediction" (pp. 518, 520) in what seems a deliberate contrast to her pursuer, the doomed Memmius—like the monk who "resisted the sacred impulse" of kneeling before the cross and so forever sealed himself off from grace's "holy light" (p. 48); and though the author cannot tell us at the end "what . . . Miriam's life [was] to be," he assures us that "Hilda had a hopeful soul, and saw sunlight on the mountaintops" (p. 522). This optimism does not altogether justify Hilda. She, too, requires "a sin to soften" her (p. 243), and, in token of her softening, must come "down from her old tower," leaving it to "another hand . . . henceforth [to] trim the lamp before the Virgin's shrine" (p. 521). But her hopefulness does serve, retrospectively, a positive function. For all Hawthorne's reticence in the matter, it throws doubt on Miriam's despair before the closed window; and despite his insistence on Hilda's "simplicity," it casts a gentler light on her judgment when, with instinctive benevolence, she helped direct a distraught friend to face her guilt, to seek mercy "from Him that hath the Spirit without measure," and thereby, perhaps, to find her dark and lonely way to redemption.

---

[12] *Parable of Ten Virgins,* Part II, 89, 88, 75, 73, 88, 89.

F. O. Matthiessen

[Hilda, Kenyon, and the "Cheerless Decay" of America]

... By turning over some of Hawthorne's unexamined assumptions, especially in *The Marble Faun*, we can get an ugly glimpse of American spiritual life, as it was destined increasingly to become in the decades after the Civil War. He clearly intended Kenyon and Hilda to be attractive: an earnest young sculptor of promise and 'quick sensibility,' who, as the era deemed appropriate, believed reverently that the girl he loved was 'a little more than mortal.' In his treatment of their relationship Hawthorne has obviously interwoven many strands of his own relations with his wife; but the unintended impression of self-righteousness and priggishness that exudes from these characters brings to the fore some extreme limitations of the standards that Hawthorne took for granted.

We need look no farther than two critical scenes with Miriam, before and after the murder of her model. In the first she has been driven by her 'weary restlessness' to visit Kenyon in his studio, in the half-formed hope that he may be able to counsel her how to escape from her desperate situation. At the sight of his Cleopatra, she is so impressed by his intuitive grasp of woman's nature that she turns impulsively to him: 'Oh, my friend, will you be my friend indeed? I am lonely, lonely, lonely. There is a secret in my heart that burns me,—that tortures me! Sometimes I fear to go mad of it; sometimes I hope to die of it; but neither of the two happens. Ah, if I could but whisper it to only one human soul!' He bids her speak, but with a hidden reserve and alarm, which her suffering can detect. For his cool reasonableness knows that if she does pour out her heart, and he then fails to respond with just the sympathy she wants, it will be worse than if she had remained silent. ' "Ah, I shall hate you!" cried she, echoing the thought which he had not spoken; she was half choked with the gush of passion that was thus turned back upon her. "You are as cold and pitiless as your own marble." '

It does no good for him to protest, as Miles Coverdale might also

---

From *American Renaissance,* pp. 356–61. Copyright 1941 by Oxford University Press, Inc. Reprinted by permission.

have done, that he is 'full of sympathy, God knows,' for his ineffectual scrupulosity has driven her away. The very evening after this
visit the terrible event takes place.

Of this event Hilda, who had turned back from the other walkers
to rejoin Miriam and Donatello, became thus unwittingly the only
observer. In deliberately creating in her the ideal innocence of a
New England girl, Hawthorne set himself to examine a nature
that, as Miriam recognizes, might endure a great burden of sorrow,
but 'of sin, not a feather's weight.' One source of Hawthorne's
knowledge of such a problem is suggested by Elizabeth Peabody's
remark that with all her sister Sophia's bravery in the face of much
suffering, 'there was one kind of thing she could not bear, and that
was, moral evil.' The result in Hilda is terrifying: Kenyon's nature
is broad as a barn in comparison. What is uppermost in the single
interview she allows herself with Miriam after the murder is her
dread that she, too, may be stained with guilt. Her dearest friend
has 'no existence for her any more,' and she wonders if she can
even talk to her 'without violating a spiritual law.'

Miriam urges, in her despair, that she is still a woman as she was
yesterday, 'endowed with the same truth of nature, the same
warmth of heart, the same genuine and earnest love, which you
have always known in me. In any regard that concerns yourself,
I am not changed . . . But, have I sinned against God and man, and
deeply sinned? Then be more my friend than ever, for I need you
more.' But as the girl recoils from her, Miriam adds: 'I always said,
Hilda, that you were merciless; for I had a perception of it, even
while you loved me best. You have no sin, nor any conception of
what it is; and therefore you are so terribly severe! As an angel,
you are not amiss; but as a human creature, and a woman among
earthly men and women, you need a sin to soften you.'

To this Hilda's only answer is that she prays God may forgive
her if she has spoken 'a needlessly cruel word,' for 'while there is a
single guilty person in the universe, each innocent one must feel
his innocence tortured by that guilt. Your deed, Miriam, has darkened the whole sky!'

To such a dazzling extreme does the daughter of the Puritans
merit Kenyon's tribute to 'the white shining purity' of her nature
as 'a thing apart.' At one point much later in the narrative she
thinks remorsefully, 'Miriam loved me well, and I failed her at her
sorest need.' But Kenyon, though observing that Hilda's unworldly
separation between the good and the bad cuts like a steel blade, and
that she is incapable of mercy since in need of none herself, still

defends to Miriam her 'just severity.' Its justice is accepted by the novelist, and even by Miriam. Yet she repeats that if Kenyon had not been cold to her confidence, if she had obeyed her first impulse, 'all would have turned out differently.' She knows too that both her friends, by their lack of active sympathy, have allowed the unreleased energies of her heart to grind destructively on herself.

The dilemma that Hawthorne has run into here through his determination to keep the scales of justice exact is due to his limited ability to create characters instead of states of mind. We can accept the position that since Miriam has sinned, or has at least been implicated in Donatello's act, her retribution must run its course. For we know that moral laws, whether under the aegis of Destiny or of Providence, are by their nature relentlessly inhuman. But what we cannot accept is that Kenyon and Hilda should be such correct mouthpieces for justice. They become thereby appallingly conscious of the significance of events in which their own human fallibility would be more confusedly involved, and they thus take on an air of insufferable superiority.

Still worse things remain to be seen in Hilda. Chilled into torpor by the fact of having to bear the knowledge of Miriam's guilt, she feels utterly alone in the Rome which Kenyon has left for the summer. In this state she begins to be drawn by the magnet of Catholicism, by its apparent comfort on all occasions for the pent-up heart. She asks herself whether its universal blessings may not belong to her as well, whether the New England faith in which she was born and bred can be perfect, 'if it leave a weak girl like me to wander, desolate, with this great trouble crushing me down?' Her struggle brings her compellingly to St. Peter's, to a confessional booth, *Pro Anglica Lingua*. But when she has poured out her whole story, and the priest asks her in some perplexity, whether, though born a heretic, she is reconciled to the Church, her answer is 'Never.' ' "And, that being the case," demanded the old man, "on what ground, my daughter, have you sought to avail yourself of these blessed privileges, confined exclusively to members of the one true Church, of confession and absolution?" '

' "Absolution, father?" exclaimed Hilda, shrinking back. "Oh no, no! I never dreamed of that! Only our Heavenly Father can forgive my sins . . ." ' This instinctive determination of Hilda's to eat her cake and have it too is, one must admit, as American as the strip-tease, of which it forms the spiritual counterpart.

To be sure, though Hilda tells the priest that she will never return to the confessional, she also says that she will hold the cathe-

dral in 'loving remembrance' as long as she lives, as the spot where
she found 'infinite peace after infinite trouble.' But by then she
has decided that it was 'the sin of others that drove me thither;
not my own, though it almost seemed so.' She has also finally begun to accept Kenyon's long hopeless love; and, at last, it is he
who turns to her for guidance, since his mind has been entangling
itself in the intricate problem of wherein Donatello has been educated and elevated by his sin. The sculptor feels that in his own
lonely life and work his thought has wandered dangerously wide,
and adds: 'Were you my guide, my counsellor, my inmost friend,
with that white wisdom that clothes you as a celestial garment,
all would go well. O Hilda, guide me home!'

She disclaims any such wisdom, but they start back to New
England together, and though she wonders what Miriam's life is
to be and where Donatello is, still 'Hilda had a hopeful soul, and
saw sunlight on the mountain-tops.' Those were the final words of
the book until Hawthorne yielded to the demand for a more explicit account of the destinies of the two who remained in Rome.
In its original form the end coincides curiously with the bright
vision in the final sentence of *Walden,* and with the rising light
that Whitman, even more than Emerson, envisaged as flooding
his America.

But the America to which Hawthorne as well as Kenyon was to
return in the year of the publication of *The Marble Faun* was
soon to be at war. Thoreau was to die of consumption during the
first year of that conflict, and shortly after its end Emerson was to
write his poem 'Terminus,' in which he intuitively foresaw the
waning of his creative powers. Hawthorne himself did not outlive
the struggle, during which, lacking Whitman's expansive faith, his
forebodings often were that 'our institutions may perish before we
shall have discovered the most precious of the possibilities which
they involve.'

The world that ensued was not one in which he could have
imagined the future careers of brittle natures like Kenyon and
Hilda, who would no doubt have been equally shocked by the success of the robber barons and by Whitman's frank avowal that the
workers alone could overthrow this predatory domination. Hawthorne recognized, in *Our Old Home,* that 'those words, "genteel"
and "ladylike," are terrible ones,' though he somewhat weakened
this observation by the tone in which he remarked that 'fineness,
subtlety, and grace' were 'that which the richest culture has

heretofore tended to develop in the happier examples of American genius, and which (though I say it a little reluctantly) is perhaps what our future intellectual advancement may make general among us.' His lack of effective resistance to that tendency was what let him be caught off guard in his creation of these lovers, who are the perfect bleached prototypes of the genteel tradition. When he was creating the world of *The Scarlet Letter*, he understood the limitations of the seventeenth century, since he could see them against the opportunities for fuller development in the democracy in which he believed. But he was not able to take the more difficult step, and to pass across in imagination from his relatively simple time and province to the dynamic transformations of American society that were just beginning to emerge.

That is not to say that Hilda's voice remains dominant even at the end of *The Marble Faun*. Although she gets the last word, Kenyon's somber reflections just before are more in keeping with the prevailing tone of the whole. He thinks that such genial natures as the Faun's 'have no longer any business on earth . . . Life has grown so sadly serious, that such men must change their nature, or else perish, like the antediluvian creatures, that required, as the condition of their existence, a more summer-like atmosphere than ours.' Melville marked that and also double-scored a passage earlier in the book where Hawthorne was meditating likewise on the theme of cheerless decay. Hawthorne was always aware of how in his Yankee world, 'no life now wanders like an unfettered stream; there is a mill-wheel for the tiniest rivulet to turn. We go all wrong, by too strenuous a resolution to go all right.' It was that competitive America to which Hawthorne, with his usual startling frankness, told Ticknor that he had no desire to come back. After his long sojourn in Europe he declared that he still loved his country: 'The United States are fit for many excellent purposes, but they certainly are not fit to live in.' . . .

Joseph C. Pattison

The Guilt of the Innocent Donatello

No reader of *The Marble Faun* questions Donatello's sinfulness: he is a murderer. What is surprising is that no one considers him guilty.[1] The image of the innocent Donatello persists despite the heinous nature of his crime and Hawthorne's otherwise unfailing concern with the moral responsibility of his characters for their acts.

The reason ordinarily assigned is the obvious fact that Donatello is the Faun. Half-animal and half-human, he is a child of nature. He has "no conscience, no remorse, no burden on the heart, no troublesome recollections of any sort; no dark future either."[2] (VI, 27–28) He tells Miriam upon recovery from her swoon, " 'I did what your eyes bade me do.' " (VI, 203) Donatello is innocent of moral choice in his act; he kills instinctively, passionately because of his love of Miriam. Indeed the guilt is Miriam's, not Donatello's. As Hilda testifies and Miriam admits, Miriam is the one who urged the murder and must be judged culpable. She understands moral issues while Donatello does not, because she is a mature being rather than a half-inhuman child of nature. So evident is this assessment that the charge that Donatello is guilty is seldom raised and his innocence is accepted without question.

The logical consequence is to conclude with R. W. B. Lewis in *The American Adam* that Donatello is "the most innocent person . . . in nineteenth-century American literature, with the exception of Billy Budd."[3] However, closer examination of Donatello's act

---

Reprinted from the *Emerson Society Quarterly,* No. 31 (II Quarter, 1963), 66–68, by permission of the *Emerson Society Quarterly.*
[1] Critics who interpret Donatello as "innocent" (of guilt, not sin) include the following: Merle E. Brown, "The Structure of *The Marble Faun,*" *AL,* XXVIII (November 1956), 302–313; Roy R. Male, *Hawthorne's Tragic Vision* (Austin, 1957), pp. 157–177; F. O. Matthiessen, *American Renaissance* (New York, 1941), pp. 308–312; Donald A. Ringe, "Hawthorne's Psychology of the Head and the Heart," *PMLA,* LXV (March 1950), 120–132; Mark Van Doren, *Hawthorne* (New York, 1949), pp. 225–231; Hyatt H. Waggoner, *Hawthorne, A Critical Study* (Cambridge, 1955), pp. 195–222.
[2] All volume and page references in my text are to *The Complete Works of Nathaniel Hawthorne,* Standard Library edition, 15 vols. (Boston, 1882).
[3] (Chicago, 1955), p. 121.

than is usually given shows that Donatello is not the epitome of innocence and that he should be contrasted to Billy rather than identified with him. Donatello is a tragic actor. Billy Budd is a tragic victim. Unlike Billy, Donatello knows enough to be free to choose. Accordingly, again in contrast to Billy, Donatello is guilty as well as sinful in his crime.

Twice Donatello is ready, even eager, to kill the model-monk who preys upon Miriam. " 'Bid me drown him! ' whispered he, shuddering between rage and horrible disgust. 'You shall hear his death-gurgle in another instant.' " (VI, 177) Miriam verbally refuses the plea made by Donatello at the Fountain of Trevi as quickly as she assents by the look in her eyes when the three later stand at the edge of Traitor's Leap. That Donatello once becomes impassioned enough in his defense of Miriam to take another's life we can accept as the spontaneous and unreflective act of a faun-like creature. But when he tries again—at a later time and another place—we may well ask if his intention was as innocent as it first seemed. The manner in which he advances to the decision is also noteworthy. On neither occasion will he kill without Miriam's consent. If this can be interpreted as inability to make a moral choice, it can also be said to have a radically different meaning: the choice is not his alone. Miriam and he must concur in the decision for the very reason that it is not innocent. If it were, Donatello would commit the murder immediately and spontaneously in the heat of his rage without consulting Miriam.

The charge of guilt is also supported by Donatello's knowledge of a change in himself prior to the murder. When Miriam rejects his proposal to drown the model-monk in the Fountain of Trevi, Donatello emits a "heavy, tremulous sigh" as he laments, " 'Methinks there has been a change upon me, these many months; and more and more, these last few days. The joy is all gone out of my life; all gone! all gone! all gone!' " (VI, 177) Donatello's fall from innocence (and consequent loss of naive joy) is not sudden; the change has taken place over the preceding "many months." What is sudden is the realization "these last few days" that the loss has taken place. Donatello is now cognizant of himself and of the fact that he differs greatly from the blithe lad of twenty who existed before love of Miriam. His self-awareness prompts a reader to glance back to his "innocent" proposal of murder and to recognize the moral growth of Donatello which is implicit in Hawthorne's portrayal of his exchange with Miriam. Even as Donatello whispers, Hawthorne comments that Donatello is "shuddering between rage and horrible disgust." Even as Miriam refuses murder, Hawthorne tells us that she seeks to soothe him, "for this naturally gentle and sportive being seemed all aflame with animal rage." (VI, 177) To the reader, Donatello *actually* shudders with rage and disgust; to Miriam, he merely *seems* to be filled with *animal* rage. The disparity is more than that between what is and what seems to be. It is that between animality and morality, between rage and disgust. For "disgust" is a moral term; it stamps the model-monk as loathesome and repugnant, or, in the words of Hawthorne a moment earlier, "repulsive and hideous." (VI, 176) The new Donatello, in short, reacts in a way which is strikingly moral and human, as the parallel to the omniscient author's own judgment attests.

Donatello's indictment of the model-monk culminates during the murder scene. " 'I did what ought to be done to a traitor!' " he exclaims to Miriam. (VI, 203) The moral judgment explicit in "ought to" and "traitor" censures the model-monk; still more, it partially justifies the man's punishment. Death by a forced plunge off Traitor's Leap was a fitting end for the traitor to Miriam. Donatello's assertion that the man had been tried and judged guilty further shows that—at the moment—he had thought the act morally just. " 'There was short time to weigh the matter; but he had his trial in that breath or two while I held him over the cliff. . .' " (VI, 204) The execution was by deliberate choice, for all the fact that the decision was fraught with passion.

But was Donatello judge as well as executioner? Donatello tells Miriam that the condemned man had " 'his sentence in that one glance, when your eyes responded to mine.' " (VI, 204) It is usually urged, as noted earlier, that Miriam passed sentence and that Donatello only did what she bade him do. However, Donatello's self-acknowledged prior loss of innocent joy, his double attempt on the man's life, his condemnation of the man in moral terms, and his insistence that there had been a trial all furnish indirect evidence that Donatello realized and was therefore responsible for what he did. Miriam's self-questioning may also be said to provide indirect evidence of Donatello's responsibility. "Had her eyes provoked or assented to this deed?" (VI, 203) Miriam's look was one of assent rather than of provocation, despite the fact that the conclusion at first appears untenable because of Hilda's admission that Miriam had a " 'look of hatred, triumph, vengeance, and, as it were, joy at some unhoped-for relief.' " (VI, 244) Direct evidence more conclusive than the eyewitness report by Hilda controverts Hilda's testimony and confirms Donatello's guilt.

The murder itself seems precluded from consideration because it took place off-stage. Yet Hawthorne surprisingly manages to make the moment of the murder the most direct and telling proof of all that Donatello was a responsible being when he killed the model-monk. Some time after the murder, while a fugitive from the law but imprisoned by his conscience, Donatello retreats to his ruined Eden, the ancestral home of the Monte Benis in the Appenines. There Kenyon visits him and makes a clay bust of his stricken friend. "By some accidental handling of the clay, entirely independent of his own will," (VI, 314) Kenyon creates a truer image of the momentarily murderous Donatello than he could or would ever fashion by his mundane conscious art.[4] It is an image that combines "animal fierceness with intelligent hatred." (VI, 314) It catches an expression by which Hilda or Miriam, both of whom witnessed the murder, "might have recognized Donatello's face as they beheld it at that terrible moment when he held his victim over the edge of the precipice." (VI, 314) The bust is complete and immutable in its revelation of the truth of the charge that Donatello was guilty, not merely sinful. It gives enduring form to the intelligence by which Donatello made the fateful choice and to his possession of that intelligence even as he poised to victimize the man whose life he held in his hands. That the bust illumines a higher and final truth is apparent in its creation independently of the artist's will. The last evidence of his guilt, the bust stands as the perfect rendering of the imperfect human clay of Donatello.

At the close, perhaps Miriam asked too much in hoping that his fall was fortunate. But she queried beyond hope in her last judgment: " 'The story of the fall of man! Is it not repeated in our romance of Monte Beni?' " (VI, 491) The romance did indeed repeat that tragic story. Donatello was not the innocent he is usually taken to be, not "the most innocent person. . . in nineteenth-century American literature, with the exception of Billy Budd." Donatello's intent was to kill. Billy Budd's act was unintentional; he simply struck back in repudiation of a charge falsely made against him. Donatello had—or thought he had—the consent of

---

[4] Taking his cue from Hawthorne's words (VI, 432), Male, *Hawthorne's Tragic Vision,* pp. 163–165, likens the human quest to sculpture—Life (clay), Death (plaster cast), Resurrection (marble). Clay sculpture combines the good and evil of human clay; plaster casts are rigid, like marble, but impure; marble sculptures are sacred, but remote from the human lot. Male then goes on to compare the specific works of sculpture and the characters in *The Marble Faun.*

the third person present. Billy astounded his onlooker, Vere, by his unsanctioned violence. Donatello was aware of changes in himself and his world. Billy was oblivious to self and baffled by the change from the world of the *Rights of Man* to that of the *Indomitable*. Donatello punished his victim after a trial; Billy, without one. Most of all, Donatello hated with intelligence—with knowledge of what he was doing—even as he committed the murder. Billy hated with feeling so inarticulate that it could express itself only by blind action. Donatello was consequently no Adam momentarily become like Billy "an angel of God" in taking the life of another. He was a wholly mortal Adam, guilty as well as sinful.

Peter D. Zivkovic

The Evil of the Isolated Intellect: Hilda, in *The Marble Faun*

The isolated individual and the aspect of evil that is attached to the isolated intellect are prominent in much of Nathaniel Hawthorne's fiction. As a theme the evil of the isolated intellect is pointedly dealt with in such tales as "Rappaccini's Daughter," "The Birthmark," "Ethan Brand," "The Man of Adamant," and "Peter Goldthwaite's Treasure." The "moral" of "Rappaccini's Daughter," for instance, is that "the power of the intellect is a power of evil unless tempered by the human affections." [1] What "The Birthmark" deals with most importantly is Aylmer's refusal to let the scope of his scientific experiments be bound by the limitations and imperfections of nature. He is obsessed with the idea of correcting human beauty—or perfecting nature. And in "Ethan Brand," we see a man who has become a monster because of an inability to perfect knowledge.

Hawthorne created these isolated protagonists deliberately and

Reprinted from *Personalist*, XLIII (Spring, 1962), 202–13, by permission of The School of Philosophy, University of Southern California.
[1] Floyd Stoval, *American Idealism* (Norman, Oklahoma, 1943), p. 67.

built his tales around the evil of their isolation. But there were two sides of Hawthorne, and while one side of him shuddered at the seeking of unnatural perfection, the other admired the goal of such a quest sufficiently to permit him to fall into the error of Hilda, in *The Marble Faun.* For Hilda, too, is certainly guilty of being an isolated individual. She, too, possesses "an obsessive desire for perfection in knowledge or virtue or art [which] has driven [her] beyond nature." [2] This type of error, in Hawthorne, is understandable. "The perpetual turning-in of the mind upon itself, the long introspective brooding over human motives, came naturally to one who lived in the shadow of a Puritan past." [3] His inhibitions robbed him of the ability truly to understand his own Hilda. She, too, is isolated. But she differs from Rappaccini, Aylmer, and Ethan Brand in that she is not deliberately made evil by Hawthorne. She differs from them in that she is not made "an accomplished but cold-hearted monster."

No, Hilda—cold-hearted though she may be—is certainly not a monster. Her intellect is evil because it is isolated, but it is isolated only because she is an inbred, a tried-and-true, Puritan. She does not deliberately attempt to soar beyond nature. Rappaccini reverses the role of God and man. He produces pure poison and pure beauty (his plants and his daughter) in a world of plants and men in which God produces only a mixture of impure poison and impure beauty. Hilda does not make things pure or perfect, she only *sees* them that way. She cannot and will not see things any other way. Marius Bewley says that "Hilda loses her innocence by proxy, as it were, when she sees her friends commit a crime." [4] But the point is that Hilda does not lose her innocence, not even by proxy. Artistically, Hawthorne wanted her to, but morally he was too stiff; he could not permit it. He isolated her, made her too perfect and too unreal. Kenyon thinks that Hilda has heard what has happened to Miriam and Donatello after their crime;

---

[2] Mark Van Doren, *Nathaniel Hawthorne* (New York, 1957), p. 139.

[3] V. L. Parrington, *Main Currents in American Thought* [The Romantic Revolution in America] (New York, 1954), p. 437. Or, putting it another way, Van Wyck Brooks says that Hawthorne "felt as if he had not lived at all, as if he were an ineffectual shadow, as if having stepped aside from the highway of human affairs, he had lost his place forever." Van Wyck Brooks, *The Flowering of New England* (New York, 1936), p. 224. Hawthorne's sympathy for Hilda, in light of his thus feeling somewhat sorry for himself, is almost reasonable.

[4] Marius Bewley, *The Complex Fate* (London, 1952), p. 46.

he says, "Then you know!—you have heard!" "Nothing," Hilda replies. "Not one word has reached my ears from the lips of any human being. Let us never speak of it again. No, no! never again." This is Hilda's weapon for combatting all evil. This is what she fights with. "Hush!" she says. "Try not to think of it!" Kenyon tells her she is "a terribly severe judge. . . . You need no mercy, and therefore know not how to show any." She replies: "But I cannot help it. It does not alter my perception of the truth." That is exactly so. Nothing alters Hilda's perception of the truth. When she sees the murder, her perception of the truth is in danger and, therefore, her very life is also in danger. "I must keep your secret, and die of it," she tells Miriam, "unless God sends me some relief by methods which are now beyond my power to imagine. It is dreadful."

The difference between such characters as Aylmer and Peter Goldthwaite, and Hilda, is that the former are villains—materialistic villains. As Judge Pyncheon is "the complete materialist, who is deluded by appearances," [5] so Hilda is the complete idealist, also deluded by appearances. They are attempting to surmount natural limitations: Hilda's is a different kind of isolation. She is orthodox idealistic, and she is good. Her *intellect* is isolated and evil, but *she* is good. It is just that she is such a brass bound idealist that for her the ideal is the real; what is unpleasant is unreal. Hawthorne wanted her to be good, but not good incarnate, which is ultimately evil. He wanted her to be only unusually good, not unbelievably good. He did not see her right. He did not recognize Hilda for what he made of her. "Melville's view of the cosmic idealist [is] a picture of the man who commits the outrageous self-centered blasphemy of judging all creation according to his own ideal, all experience by a predetermining assumption." [6] This is as true of Hawthorne as it is of Melville, when Hawthorne sees right, as he did when he created Ethan Brand, Goldthwaite, Rappaccini. But he was blinded by Hilda. She was what the Puritan in him wanted her to be, and he failed to temper her with a fault: thus he damned her with the greatest of all faults.

---

[5] Richard Harter Fogle, *Hawthorne's Fiction* (Norman, 1952), p. 132.
[6] Milton R. Stern, ed., *Herman Melville's* TYPEE *and* BILLY BUDD (New York, 1958), p. xiii. Elsewhere Stern expresses this idea similarly, in his wild and exciting book, *The Fine Hammered Steel of Herman Melville* (Urbana, 1958), p. 248: "Hawthorne, with his Goodman Browns and Birthmarks . . . recoiled in horror from the last, last crime of soul suicide, which is always the removal of self from common humanity."

Several of the more astute Hawthorne critics have suggested that Hilda, the blond, pure artist (significantly a copyist-artist) in *The Marble Faun,* is more or less a depiction of the writer's wife, Sophia.[7] Certainly such a comparison is justifiable, at least on one level. Hilda is surely as righteous, as virtuous, and as pure, and even as "painfully high-minded" as was Sophia. And Hawthorne goes far out of his way to paint a picture of Hilda's virginal purity. He has Miriam, who knows her best, say that Hilda "would die of her first wrongdoing—supposing for a moment that she could be capable of doing wrong." Elsewhere Miriam refers to her as the "saintlike Hilda," and wishes that she could choose to remain "spotless in the estimation of her white-souled friend" and not be absolutely resigned, as a human being, to accept "infamy in the eyes of the whole world." Hilda is, of course, altogether too pure, too virginal, and too ideal. And although this fact is generally recognized and acknowledged, it is not always properly interpreted. Charles Feidelson, for example, speaks of the "Simple morality of Hilda, a purely allegorical creature equipped with white robe, tower, lamp, and doves." [8] And Hyatt Waggoner says that she appears to be "the embodiment of nineteenth-century feminism, sentimentalism, and the 'religion of the heart.' She is 'pure,' 'spiritual,' the guardian of moral values. . ." [9] Such observations are quite accurate and valid, as far as they go. But they go wrong in so far as they tend to pigeonhole Hilda too easily as an end, and in so far, that is, as they too casually dismiss her and fail to recognize the importance of her potential as a means to a very significant end: the end of the evil that is attached to the isolated intellect in Hawthorne's fictional universe.

We must not fail to take into account that Hawthorne's characters are invariably evil (or at least tinted with evil) whenever they are too much of anything. In Hawthorne, always, "a fatality attaches to creatures too richly endowed." R. H. Fogle observes that "Hilda represents for [Hawthorne] a real, valuable, and attractive aspect of human life. . . . He believes that there are such women as she . . . that they are significant and representative." But as Waggoner had pointed out earlier, "Hawthorne could not draw the type [Phoebe, Hilda, Priscilla] 'realistically' be-

---

[7] Malcom Cowley, ed., *Viking Portable Hawthorne* (New York, 1948), p. 14; Fogle, p. 173; F. O. Matthiessen, *American Renaissance* (New York, 1941), p. 356; Hyatt H. Waggoner, *Hawthorne* (Cambridge, 1955), p. 237.
[8] Charles Feidelson, *Symbolism and American Literature* (Chicago, 1953), p. 15.
[9] Waggoner, p. 202.

cause 'in his heart' he did not really believe in her ... because the type doesn't exist in nature." [10] And on an even more important level Fogle errs in not reading enough into the character of Hilda. He says, "One must feel ... that Hawthorne was mistaken in making her the center of interest for a long section of the book. ... Hilda cannot act, but is only acted upon, since action is imperfection." [11] What Fogle misses here is the fact that Hilda *is* a character of action which is something more than imperfect; her action is a conscious and determined endeavor to remain untouched by human society—to maintain her individual, isolated virginal purity in the midst of all the earthly evils of social intercourse, in the midst of all the mud and dirt of ordinary humanity. Waggoner is correct when he says that "in his heart" Hawthorne did not believe in Hilda. But—and this is the important point—for the duration of *The Marble Faun*, he did believe in her.

When Hilda sees Donatello kill the monk-shadow (at Miriam's instigation), she withdraws as completely as she can from basic human conditions. "Never before," Hawthorne tells us, "had this young ... spirit known what it is to be despondent. It was the unreality of the world that made her so." It is not the *unreality* but rather the *reality* of the world which causes Hilda's shock, her despondency. Hawthorne has lost sight of what he intended to do, for at this point he is perfectly serious—he makes Hilda's morality the measure of reality. When Miriam visits Hilda, after the former's "great sin," Hilda's "first impulse" is to forbid her ex-friend's entrance. She finally admits Miriam, however, but tells her not to come nearer. Miriam asks, "Are we not friends?" "No, no!" Hilda emphatically replies. "Am I not the same as yesterday?" Miriam persists. Hilda shudders and says, "Alas, no," and thus symbolically rejects all ties with ordinary mortality and everyday morality.

This scene, perhaps better than any other in the book, illustrates the basic, human contrasts between Miriam and Hilda—and Miriam emerges far superior to all perceptive readers (as I see it, and not, as Waggoner suggests, only to the modern reader).

Essential truths of the human situation are exactly what Hawthorne's imagination could not shrink from—not even ... when he wanted to. Nor does his matured conception of art neglect the

---

[10] Waggoner, p. 172.
[11] Fogle, p. 98.

"real" for the "ideal"; it posits the relation that he believed should exist between them.[12]

Matthiessen gives Hawthorne too much credit here. What he says is almost true of Hawthorne at his best. But it surely is not a general truth. If Hawthorne had had the courage of his convictions, one of his feminine characters might have become—as Hester hoped to become—"the prophetess to establish the whole relation between man and woman on a surer ground of mutual happiness." *The Scarlet Letter* would have been an even more successful novel, and Hester a more believable character, if Hawthorne had not negated the logic of his plot by declaring that Hester now felt her act to be unholy and herself "stained with sin." "Having renounced experience," in this, his greatest book, "Hawthorne returned in his later novels to describe the victory of the blonde principle of purity." [13]

In *The Marble Faun* Hawthorne has returned with a vengeance to the victory of his blonde women, to the Puritanical. Hawthorne knew what sin and life were all about. But the older he got the less he liked the truth, the more he was frightened by it. In an early story, "Fancy's Show Box," he gives an explicit statement of his artistic perception: the moral conclusion he gives us in this story is that "Man must not disclaim his brotherhood, even with the guiltiest, since though his hand be clean, his heart has surely been polluted by the flitting phantoms of iniquity." This is Hawthorne's truth, and it is an admirable one. But it is what he missed in his final complete novel; it is what he forgot when he created Hilda.

Not knowing is bad enough, in Hawthorne's scheme of things. He devotes almost the entirety of one of his best pieces of writing to pointing out the dangers to which the innocent character is exposed. Robin, in "My Kinsman, Major Molineaux," is forced to struggle with numerous temptations and pitfalls because of his innocence—temptations and pitfalls the potential perils and hazards of which are increased tenfold simply because he does not know.[14] This sort of innocence, this sort of isolation, of itself,

---

[12] Matthiessen, p. 263.
[13] Frederic I. Carpenter, "Puritans Preferred Blondes," *The New England Quarterly*, IX (June, 1936), 262.
[14] For a fine explication of these ideas, see S. L. Gross's article, "History as Moral Adventure," *Nineteenth-Century Fiction*, XII (September, 1957), 97–109.

is only a condition: a pathetic, a tragic condition, but unless self-imposed it is not an evil condition. And the character who does not know can only be sympathized with, to a certain extent, *if* his not knowing is a result of innocence, and if this innocence is not carried too far. But even this unknowing character becomes real only when and if he begins to know; he becomes a true character only in so far as he becomes morally aware, and therefore morally believable. He realizes himself, and we as readers are able truly to realize him as a character, to whatever extent he achieves—or at least begins to achieve—moral wisdom. The character who deliberately refuses to learn, who deliberately refuses to permit himself to benefit from the experiences that are available to him, is guilty of rejecting moral participation. He sins, that is, by deliberately refusing to accept the realities of his own earthly and moral existence; and he is guilty, ultimately, of the great sin of isolation-which-is-blasphemy. Hawthorne says, "We struggle forth...bruised and bewildered. We stare wildly about us, and discover—[and here he subtly gives us Hilda] or it may be, we never make the discovery—that it was not actually the sky that has tumbled down, but merely a frail structure of our own rearing, which...has fallen because we founded it on nothing." Hilda's "frail structure" is "founded on nothing," certainly, but it never falls. She refuses to permit it to fall.

Hilda is like the Sunshine wine of Monte Beni. Kenyon says that the promise of this wine's fragrance "is like the airy sweetness of youthful hopes, that no realities will ever satisfy." This can be said of Hilda's fragrance, also. And Kenyon adds, "The finest [of other wines] is vulgar in comparison," just as, as Kenyon chooses to look at it, the finest of other people would be vulgar in comparison to Hilda. But we must not, of course, stop with Kenyon's observations. We must pay attention to such words as those of the old butler of Monte Beni—Tomaso, who represents truth and time and tradition. This venerable character, "with a shrewd twinkle in his eye," tells Kenyon that his observations are partly true.

> But to speak all the truth [he adds], there is another excellent reason why neither a cask nor a flask of our precious vintage should ever be sent to market...[it] is so fond of its native home, that a transportation of even a few miles turns it quite sour. And yet it is a wine that keeps well in the cellar, underneath this floor, and gathers fragrance, flavor, and brightness, in its dark dungeon.

Hilda is equally fond of her "native home." She "would sleep securely in her old Roman tower," and she "anticipated many months of lonely, but unalloyed enjoyment," in this, her own "dark dungeon." And she, too, "should [n]ever be sent to market": "keeping a maiden heart within her bosom, she rejoiced in the freedom that enabled her still to choose her own sphere and dwell in it . . . without another inmate."

Hilda's differences with and from Miriam are interesting. We are told that Hilda "had a faculty . . . of ignoring all moral blotches in a character that won her admiration. She purified the objects of her regard by the mere act of turning such spotless eyes upon them. (This is, incidentally, an excellent example of Hilda's absolute perception of unreality.) But Hilda can only ignore the moral blotches so long as she can successfully control her perception, so long as she can delude herself into thinking that the moral blotches do not exist. She is unable to reconcile her accidental witnessing of Miriam's sin with her conception of Miriam's soul, and thus she chooses to sever the bond of their relationship. Miriam tries to save the friendship (and, at the same time, Hilda):

> Are we not friends? I loved you dearly! I love you still! . . . I am a woman . . . endowed with the same truth of nature, the same warmth of heart . . . which you have always known in me. . . . Have I deceived you? Then cast me off! Have I wronged you personally? Then forgive me, if you can. But, have I sinned against God and man. . . . Then be more my friend than ever, for I need you more.

But Hilda rejects this very human plea, and tells Miriam that she would discolor the "pure, white atmosphere, in which I try to discern what things are good and true." Miriam is aware of Hilda's great error, here, and, rising to the occasion, forgives her for what she realizes is a greater sin than her own. "Let it pass," she says. "I, whose heart it has smitten upon, forgive you." Later, Miriam is completely aware that Hilda's purity is unreal, and evil, and pities her for all that. And here she sees better than does Hawthorne. "I never questioned" the white purity of Hilda's nature, Miriam says; although "when she cast me off, it severed some few remaining bonds between me and decorous womanhood. But were there anything to forgive, I do forgive her."

There can be no doubt of Miriam's rightness and Hilda's

wrongness, in this conflict. Hawthorne always felt that "attainment of security at the expense of involvement was a distorting escape from what was morally curative in the struggle for human fulfilment." [15] Miriam and Donatello, the two characters in *The Marble Faun* who become most involved, are also the two characters who come closest to human fulfilment. It is Miriam, for instance, who sees through the picture of the Archangel, and is really indirectly including Hilda in her criticism, when she says:

> With what half-scornful delicacy he sets his prettily sandalled foot on the head of his prostrate foe! Is it thus that virtue looks the moment after its death struggle with evil? No, no; I could have told Guido better ... the Archangel's feathers should have been torn from his wings ... all ruffled, till they looked like Satan's own! His sword should be streaming with blood ... his armor crushed, his robes rent, his breast gory.... He should press his foot hard down upon the old serpent, as if his very soul depended upon it ... the battle never was such child's play as Guido's dapper Archangel seems to have found it.

Thus, Miriam sees and verbalizes the problem of the novel.

Even Kenyon, a relatively unreal character, perceives that Donatello's mishap is proof that life is too serious and too sinful for anyone to remain completely innocent and untouched through it. Kenyon compares Donatello to Adam, who "fell that we might ultimately rise to a far loftier paradise than his." And he tells Hilda, "what a mixture of good there may be in things evil," and that "the greatest criminal, if you look at his conduct from his own point of view ... may seem not so unquestionably guilty, after all." But Hilda, with great consistency, cannot bear such ideas. She is too hopeful, too pure, too unattached, to derive any conclusion but evil from Donatello's and Miriam's sin. Once again Hilda goes "all wrong, by too strenuous a resolution to go all right." But this time she takes Kenyon with her, in her wrong direction. "There is ... only one right and one wrong," she tells him; "and I do not understand, and may God keep me from ever understanding, how two things so totally unlike can be mistaken for one another; nor how two mortal foes, as Right and Wrong surely are, can work together in the same deed." Kenyon had begun to see, but is stopped by Hilda in the midst of his

---

[15] S. L. Gross, "Hawthorne and the Shakers," *American Literature,* XXIX (January, 1958), p. 457.

perception. And this is quite typical, it seems to me, of Hawthorne's mishandling of both Hilda and Kenyon throughout much of the novel. Kenyon sees Hilda's evil, yet loves her and begs her to guide him. He perceives, and is involved (he "participates"); and with Donatello and Miriam he is part of a "linked circle of three, with many reminiscences and forebodings flashing through their hearts." Miriam and Donatello go off to repent and be punished, and to live their lives of sadness. Kenyon, for Hilda's sake, turns away from life. He glosses over his own perception, his involvement, and chooses an existence of withdrawal. Although he has "seen," and lets Hilda know that he has seen, he "shocks" her "beyond words," and so renounces his perceptive faculty, and says, "Forgive me, Hilda. I never did believe it."

Many prominent characters in Hawthorne's most important work, then, are characters involved in the evil of the isolated intellect: Rappaccini, Ethan Brand, Aylmer, Wakefield, Richard Digby in the tales; Westervelt, Judge Pyncheon, Chillingworth in the novels. Most of these characters are materialists who are deluded by appearances, and are, as a result, wrongheaded in their placement of values. Hilda is equally wrongheaded in her self-delusion, and her misrepresentation of appearances; and although she is not guilty in the same way, she is guilty to a similar degree. The sole important difference is that Hilda is a complete idealist rather than a complete materialist. While she does not have the same driving, powerful force of imposed evil, she is as resolute in her isolation as any of these characters. While her idealism is internal whereas their idealization of materialism is external, the *purity* of her isolation goes as far as theirs—or farther. That is, unlike Rappaccini and Judge Pyncheon, Hilda does not attempt to impose her will on, and alter, circumstances. Instead, more like Wakefield and Digby, she willfully withdraws from circumstances, and refuses to permit them to alter her; and—again like Digby—she turns to stone (but only figuratively).

Waggoner makes an observation which is less directly concerned, on the surface, with the ideas of this paper, but an observation which, nevertheless, carries with it a great deal of implicit significance. "Hawthorne saw the skull beneath the skin," he tells us, "and realized the truth of E. A. Robinson's phrase, 'how little we have to do with what we are.' " [16] Hilda's wrong-

---

[16] Waggoner, *Tales,* p. xv.

minded perception is that she would fail to realize the truth of such a phrase. Her main weakness stems from the fact that she tries too hard to control what she is. And because she could not have realized the truth of this statement of Robinson's, she could easily become the objectification of the moral that is found elsewhere in Robinson. A stanza in his poem, "The Children of Night," reads:

> 'T were better, ere the sun go down
> Upon the first day we embark,
> In life's imbittered sea to drown,
> Than sail forever in the dark.

Roy R. Male

The Transfiguration of Figures: *The Marble Faun*

Many readers, even those who appreciate Hawthorne's other works, have found *The Marble Faun* slow going. Its defects as a novel have often been observed.[1] No coherent structure is immediately apparent; particularly in the opening chapters, Hawthorne is guilty of awkward transitions and clumsy playful author-to-reader comments; the narrative seems to bog down in the lengthy descriptions of Rome and its art objects. Of the four characters, only Miriam and Donatello show any signs of vitality. To make matters worse, Hawthorne teases the reader into looking at the wrong side of the tapestry; he supplies clues about Miriam and the model, for instance, that prompt precisely the kind of investigation he deplores in the conclusion.

From *Hawthorne's Tragic Vision*, pp. 157–77. Copyright © 1957 by The University of Texas Press. Reprinted by permission of W. W. Norton & Company, Inc., and Roy R. Male. [Textual citations are to the Riverside Edition of Hawthorne's works, ed. George Parsons Lathrop.]
[1] See Waggoner, *Hawthorne*, pp. 201–207; Mark Van Doren, *Hawthorne* (William Sloane Associates, New York, 1949), pp. 226–30.

The book's almost complete failure as a novel inevitably limits its worth as romance, and I think *The Marble Faun* must finally be reckoned the least successful of Hawthorne's finished works. Yet with all its defects, the book deserves a sympathetic rereading, since its complex framework embraces Hawthorne's fullest explorations of morality and art. Indeed, its shortcomings result mainly from the grandeur of his aim. Never before had he tried to achieve so much in his medium; never before had he pressed the romance to its breaking point, as he does with Hilda in this book. His own comments reflect this gap between achievement and goal. "The thing is a failure," he said, in a mood of despair; yet he also called *The Marble Faun* his "best work."

Hawthorne's subject, once again, is the "riddle of the soul's growth" (VI, 434). How does man develop his full human potential? How do incarnation, conversion, transfiguration take place? The central figures in this process are already familiar to us: the young man who frolics in timeless spatial freedom and innocence; the woman inexorably linked with time and guilt but also with a redemptive ideal; and the union between them, with its attendant shocks and recognitions. In *The House of the Seven Gables* Hawthorne involved the individual with his immediate cultural and familial ancestry; here he plunges the innocent into all time, confronts him with the totality of the past and with the very "model," the prototype of evil.

Some of Hawthorne's difficulties resulted from his efforts to achieve a density he felt to be lacking in his earlier work. In this book he strove to make the observer-commentator, Kenyon, a more substantial figure than Miles Coverdale; he tried to make Hilda both an allegorical ideal and a character; and he aimed at fusing action and setting in a structure more complex than any he had hitherto attempted. In this last intention he was quite successful, though the book's structure is discernible only after careful reading.

As the opening and concluding chapters indicate, the book is about four characters—Miriam, Hilda, Kenyon, and Donatello—who undergo a threefold process of transformation. The simplest way of grasping the book's structure is to envisage a circle divided into four parts revolving about a center. This center, or central experience, is expressed in various ways throughout the book. It is the way of conversion, in art and in life. Hawthorne discerns a "threefold analogy,—the clay model, the Life; the plaster cast, the Death; and the sculptured marble, the Resurrection" (VI, 432). Indeed, all of Rome itself seems designed after this analogy. Its grimy streets swarm with intricate, colorful life; its pavements cover a grave; and its towers and churches stretch heavenward. "Everywhere . . . a Cross,—and nastiness at the foot of it" (VI, 135).

The history of Rome and its environs follows the same pattern. The first stage was the innocent "sylvan life of Etruria, while Italy was yet guiltless of Rome"; the second was the sin and fall of Rome; the third, of course, was the rise of Christianity from the labyrinthine depths of the fall. These three periods are marked by cultural "peaks": Etruria in the Faun of Praxiteles in Chapter I; Rome in the statue of Marcus Aurelius in Chapter XVIII (which is entitled "On the Edge of the Precipice" and concludes with the "fall" of the model and of Donatello); and Christianity in the statue of Pope Julius in Chapter XXXV.

To combine the four characters and the threefold process is to arrive at the mystic number seven, which receives much attention in the book. The seven-branched candlestick that was lost at the Ponte Moll during Constantine's reign suggests to Hilda "an admirable idea for a mystic story or parable, or seven-branched allegory, full of poetry, art, philosophy, and religion" (VI, 422). The whole ritual of transformation is summed up in Miriam's bridal gift to Hilda, an Etruscan bracelet, "the connecting bond of a series of seven wondrous tales, all of which, as they were dug out of seven sepulchres, were characterized by a seven-fold sepulchral gloom." In its "entire circle," the bracelet is the symbol of a "sad mystery," though there is a gleam of hope at the end.

In someone else's fiction we might dismiss these recurrent allusions to a seven-branched allegory as idle fancy, but Hawthorne seldom if ever labors a point unless it has meaning. Looking back over the book, we discover that every seventh chapter contains a recognition scene in which an individual is transfigured by a vital bond with the past. These sacramental "rites" do not follow the orthodox order prescribed by the Roman Catholics, nor do we expect them to. What Hawthorne does insist upon is the real presence of the past and the need for communion with it if transformation is to occur. The first of these scenes occurs, of course, in Chapter I, when the three artists detect Donatello's striking resemblance to the statue and name him the "very Faun of Praxiteles." In Chapter VII Hilda is startled to observe that Miriam's expression has become almost exactly that of Beatrice Cenci. The corpse of the dead Capuchin, with the blood oozing from its nostrils, assumes the likeness of all evil for Miriam in Chapter XXI. It symbolizes "the deadly iteration with which she was doomed to behold the image of her crime reflected back upon her in a thousand ways" (VI, 222). By this time Donatello has assumed a similar burden from the past, and his new awareness of its weight is typified in Chapter XXVIII when he takes up the alabaster skull of his ancestor and explains its meaning to Kenyon. Having done penance, Miriam and Donatello find their union blessed at "high noon" in Chapter XXXV, when the statue of Pope Julius seems to become "endowed with spiritual life." It is now Hilda's turn to recognize the bond, and in Chapter XLII she realizes for the first time the harshness of her earlier attitude toward Miriam. Now she is able to see the resemblance between herself and her former friend, and she makes what amounts to a penitential journey to the Palazzo Cenci, haunted by the "lovely shade of Beatrice."

The final "incarnation" takes place during the magnificent carnival scene of Chapter XLIX. Though Kenyon has been intellectually aware of the past, he has cherished a spiritual love for Hilda that has insulated him from the shocks of vital experience; he has resisted any real involvement with Miriam's trouble; and he has retreated from her suggested analogy between their story and the Fall of man. Now, in spite of himself, he becomes a part of the carnival. He finds his Hilda only after an exaggerated re-enactment of the Fall of man. A giant Eve, a female figure "seven feet tall," singles out the sculptor and makes "a ponderous assault on his heart." Failing in her first attempts, she shoots him in the heart with a popgun, "covering Kenyon with a cloud of lime-dust" (VI, 504). This affair is "like a feverish dream," a surrealistic version of Adam's reduction to human clay, but it qualifies Kenyon for union with the multifoliate rosebud, the spirit incarnate in Hilda.

As the characters in the book are gradually driven toward recognition of their resemblance to figures in timeless myth, the reader's insight simultaneously deepens to perceive the relation of *The Marble Faun* to the literary tradition. Miriam is linked not only with Beatrice Cenci and Cleopatra but also with Eve, the Biblical Miriam, Jael, Judith, and Rachel. Donatello (Hawthorne seems to have given him this name because he recognized the Italian sculptor as an authentic primitive)[2] is linked with Adam before the Fall and with Cain after his crime. The pure innocence of Hilda has its historic counterparts in the Virgin Mary and in the saint whose name she shares (VI, 71).

---

[2] See Hawthorne's reference to Donatello (X,345).

As might be expected, echoes of Milton reverberate throughout the book. In the sculptor's studio Miriam discovers the "grand, calm head" of the great Puritan poet, a figure that could have been shaped only through "long perusal and deep love" of *Paradise Lost* and Milton's other poems. Surely we should take this as Hawthorne's own tribute to one who had preceded him in probing deep into man's universal nature. Immediately behind Miriam and Donatello stand the eternal woman and man in Milton's story of the Fall: the woman's yearning for further knowledge, her effort to achieve increased efficiency through division of labor— her desire, in short, to "know" the man; the man's initial unity with nature, his impassioned longing for a mate, and his "glorious trial of exceeding love" as he joins Eve in sin. The last four books of *Paradise Lost* remain the best introduction to Hawthorne.

The links with Shakespeare are less obvious but almost as important. The model, Miriam, Donatello, and Hilda are haunted by an indelible bloodstain that reminds us of Lady Macbeth's tortured efforts to cleanse her hands. In dealing with the contagiousness of evil, Hawthorne may have called to mind the dank, graveyard atmosphere of *Hamlet,* where the dram of evil infests all the noble substance of mankind. There is something rotten in Rome as in Denmark; the skulls of the Capuchins and the corpse of Brother Antonio are reminiscent of Yorick and of Polonius at supper. "To Kenyon's morbid view, there appeared to be a contagious element rising foglike from the ancient depravity of Rome, and brooding over the dead and half-rotten city" (VI, 468). The impact of this atmosphere on the sculptor faintly resembles Hamlet's second and fourth soliloquies: "I am sluggish," Kenyon mutters; "a weak, nerveless fool, devoid of energy and promptitude." It takes all his energy to fling aside this mood of "morbid hesitation."

But Kenyon is not Prince Hamlet, nor was he meant to be. He is an attendant, an adviser, full of high sentence, and at times almost the Fool. Thus, as Matthiessen has observed, Hawthorne looks backward to Milton and forward to Eliot,[3] and not so much to Prufrock as to the *Four Quartets.* For *The Marble Faun* is concerned with the ways in which nature and spirit, innocence and evil, time and eternity may be conquered and reconciled in a moment of incarnation. Eliot's dove and rose are, of course, far

---

[3] Matthiessen discusses different parallels but comes to the same conclusion. *American Renaissance,* pp. 351–68.

removed from Hawthorne's, but the central experience is much
the same. Eliot links spiritual conversion with poetry and music;
Hawthorne unites it with sculpture and romance.

In *The Marble Faun,* the parallel between sculpture and life is
introduced in the title, established in the first paragraph, and
maintained throughout the book. The process of transfiguration is
as central in art as it is in life. The three stages of sculpture—clay,
plaster cast, and marble—are, as we have already noted, analogous
to life, death, and resurrection. Hawthorne begins by describing
the marble statues in the sculpture room at the Capitol, "shining
in the undiminished majesty and beauty of their ideal life," but at
the same time "corroded by the damp earth." In the statue of a
child "clasping a dove to her bosom, but assaulted by a snake" is
prefigured the choice between "Innocence or Evil"—a choice that
will affect the lives of the four individuals standing in the room.

The whole problem of evil, of reconciling "the incongruity of
Divine Omnipotence and outraged, suffering Humanity," is in
fact summed up in Kenyon's natural comparison of God to a
sculptor who "held the new, imperfect earth in his hand, and
modelled it" (VI, 305). In creating the world, God was subject
to the limitations of his art form, the imperfect clay in which he
worked. Clay is, as Miriam says, earthy and human. Kenyon's
clay model captures "all Cleopatra—fierce, voluptuous, passionate,
tender, wicked, terrible, and full of poisonous and rapturous enchantment." His clay bust of Donatello similarly expresses the
mixture of good and evil that characterizes human life. Flexible,
warm, impure, the intricate shape of clay seems "more interesting
than even the final marble, as being the intimate production of the
sculptor himself, moulded throughout with his loving hands, and
nearest to his imagination and heart" (VI, 140).

The beauty and life of the clay model disappear in the
plaster cast. Imbued with mortality, it has no celestial hopes;
it has the rigidity of marble with none of its purity. The skull
in Donatello's room is carved "in gray alabaster, most skillfully
done to the death, with accurate imitation of the teeth, the su-
tures, the empty eye-caverns, and the fragile little bones of the
nose." The corpse of the dead Capuchin congeals into a ghastly
waxen hardness that fits it into this grisly category. Like the ma-
cabre skulls in the Capuchin cemetery, the corpse seems a malevo-
lent mockery of man's hopes for a future life.

But out of the clay and the plaster emerges the pure, white,

undecaying figure done in marble, which assumes a sacred character. "It insures immortality to whatever is wrought in it, and therefore makes it a religious obligation to commit no idea to its mighty
guardianship, save such as may repay the marble for its faithful
care, its incorruptible fidelity, by warming it with an ethereal life"
(VI, 163). Yet though the marble should resolve the feverish
activity of life into a cool repose—"a blessed change," as Miriam
calls it—too often it appears rigid, harsh, and remote from human
concerns. "You are as cold and pitiless as your own marble," she
exclaims, as she detects Kenyon's reluctance to become entangled
in her affairs.

With this basic resemblance between sculpture and moral growth
established, we may now proceed to Hawthorne's distinction between sculpture and painting. Sculpture, as he views it in this
book, is essentially a masculine art form. It freezes an image in
space and has nothing temporal about it. "Flitting moments,"
Kenyon observes, "ought not to be incrusted with the eternal
repose of marble" (VI, 31). A sculptural subject, therefore, ought
to be in a "moral standstill." Painting, on the other hand, is essentially feminine. "Your frozen art," Miriam gibes, "has nothing
like the scope and freedom of Hilda's and mine. In painting there
is no similar objection to the representation of brief snatches of
time." Painting, she adds, is a warmer, more heartfelt medium.

The man, therefore, is a sculptor, while the two women are
painters. But the fact that Hilda is a "copyist" requires further
comment if we are to understand the initial artistic situation. To
put it schematically, at the outset Donatello is nature, Hilda is
spirit, and Miriam and Kenyon are the two working artists. Donatello, obviously, is the object: he is all matter, though a spiritual
potential may be discerned. Hilda, as spirit, sees *sub specie aeterni-
tatis*. She looks right through the surface of paintings to the central point or aim of the artist; she works religiously; but she can
create nothing new. Donatello is the origin, Hilda the "end." To be
converted into art, Donatello must "unearth"; Hilda must "earth-
stain." Viewed from this perspective, the crucial moment comes
late in the book when Donatello unearths the earth-stained statue
of Venus de' Medici—a statue that reminds Kenyon of his quest
for Hilda.

Truly creative art, therefore, requires both penetrative insight
and sympathetic investment. Without the humane clothing of a
sympathetic imagination, penetrative insight is like rigorous Freud-
ian literary criticism; it plumbs the surface, but it leaves us with a

nude, or at its worst, with a skull. On Hilda's religious plane it results simply in a pure copy of an unchanging idea. But investment
without insight produces mechanical superficial copies far inferior
to Hilda's spiritual imitations. Transformation of material into art
must ultimately remain a mystery, a miracle. Like human conversion, it is consummated in a moment of immediate apprehension
that comes as a reward for intellectual discipline and sympathetic
understanding. The final product, the "genial moment" in which
the inner germ finds the perfection of its outward form, is not
entirely preconceived. With both his Cleopatra and his bust of
Donatello, Kenyon begins hopefully with his conscious intentions,
lives through a period of despair, and finally achieves the vital
expression "independent of his own will."

This, I take it, is the way in which Hawthorne transformed his
own "blocks of material" taken from his notebooks. We have to
remember, however, that the notebook passages themselves were
not simply raw material, recorded at random from Hawthorne's
experience. Selected in the first place because they might bear
upon the theme of a future romance, many of these passages
were sufficiently "worked up" so that they needed little alteration
when placed in the context of his book. Like the fragments of
Venus de' Medici, they assume a new life and light when joined
with "the whole figure." Hawthorne's comments on nude statuary,
for instance, seem merely naïve and provincial when read in the
French and Italian Notebooks. But when voiced by Miriam and
Kenyon, they are illuminated by "the whole figure" of the book.
In a fallen world, the chaste nudity of innocence must be clothed
by time and tragedy before conversion can occur.

The discussions of art can be fully understood only as part of
the book's thematic structure. Its action we have outlined as an
ever widening four-part circle, revolving about a three-fold central
experience. After rebelling against her destined role as woman,
Miriam discovers her bond with time and the specter of guilt;
Donatello becomes passionately entangled with Miriam and her
guilt; Hilda becomes involved (though vicariously) with Miriam,
Donatello, and their guilt; and finally Kenyon (in an even more
diluted mode) recognizes his relation to Miriam, Donatello, Hilda,
and the total burden of humanity.

It is fitting that Miriam should be the major figure in the first
part of the book, for she potentially offers what Rome does—"all
time." A prototype of womanhood like Beatrice Rappaccini, Hester,
and Zenobia, she seems to contain all races in her rich, mysterious

origins. There is "an ambiguity about this young lady": linked like Eve and Pandora to the very model of evil, she also bears the seed of maturity and benediction. She seems so large and bounteous in this archetypal role that it comes as a shock to read her assumed name: "Miriam Schaeffer, artist in oils." Her studio in the castle, like the rooms of the other characters, is a projection of her inner traits; it is "the outward type of a poet's imagination." In it are two kinds of sketches that clearly reveal her ambiguity. One is a group of scriptural subects, showing again and again the idea of "a woman acting the part of revengeful mischief towards man" (VI, 61); the other is a series of domestic scenes, representing the "earthly paradise" that results from "wedded affection" and the newborn child. Miriam intuitively knows what Zenobia was finally forced to recognize: that "woman must strike through her own heart to reach a human life." The two groups of sketches thus illustrate "the life that belongs to woman."

At the outset, however, Miriam has rebelled against this life. She pictures herself as a figure apart, and in all the accounts supplied in her immediate background the one common element is her attempt to break the bond. Her original "crime," however, cannot be washed away or painted over. We know that her mother died when Miriam was an infant and that a marriage unsuitable for the daughter but convenient for the family fortunes had been arranged. Miriam's fiancé had been her cousin, a man whose character "betrayed traits so evil, so treacherous, so vile, and yet so strangely subtle, as could only be accounted for by the insanity which often develops itself in old, close-kept races of men, when long unmixed with newer blood" (VI, 487). She revolted against her father, repudiating the marriage contract. Then followed the nameless crime (probably, judging from the parallel with Beatrice Cenci, the murder of her father). Though innocent of legal guilt, Miriam was emotionally implicated in the crime, since her cousin clearly was the criminal. It is he who reappears in the catacombs, a spectral personification of evil and guilt. The model knew Miriam as a young girl (VI, 116, 223); that he is her former fiancé and cousin is clearly implied when she observes in retrospect that he must have been a madman. "Insanity must have been mixed up with his original composition, and developed by those very acts of depravity which it suggested" (VI, 488).

Legally innocent but morally guilty, affianced to satanic evil, Miriam obviously bears more than casual resemblance to Eve after her first depravity. Her original crime, like Eve's, was rebellion

against the father ("Miriam" originally meant "rebellion"). Like
Hester and Zenobia, however, she is linked not only to guilt but
also to the vessel of purification; she is potentially a second Eve
(again her name is significant: "Mary," of course, derives from
Greek "Mariam," Hebrew "Miryam"). Hilda is Miriam's closest
friend; they are like "sisters of the same blood," containing between
them the essence of womanhood. But unlike Pearl, who is Hester's
seed and effectively bruises the head of the serpent, Hilda does not
function very well as a narrative embodiment of woman's redemptive qualities. We note the meaning of her separation from Miriam
and their eventual reunion, but it is not dramatically convincing.

Miriam's efforts to expunge her guilt, to find "new hopes, new
joys," can only lead to further extension of her Original Sin. Once
the man has fixed his lot with her, he is, as Milton says, "certain to
undergo like doom." Donatello, whose transformation appropri-
ately occupies the central portion of the book, is first introduced as
the ultimate of primitive innocence. Free to gambol in space, he
"has nothing to do with time" (VI, 29). In his animal-like youth,
he enjoys the peak of intuitive sympathy with all forms of life. In
order to mature, he must be educated through the heart by Miriam.
But he educates her as well. She needs the ritual of the romp
through the Borghese Eden, a refreshment from the fountain of
simplicity in order to assume her proper role as woman. When she
asks why he follows her, he answers simply, "Because I love you."
There is no other way to say it, and he saves her from moving into
a brittle existence where such sentiments, if uttered at all, would
be verbalized into something like, "Our emotional impulses are in-
tegrated, and we show promise of attaining a moral and intellectual
continuum." He saves her, in short, from the rigid refinement of a
Kenyon.

The first fruit of Donatello's "marriage" with Miriam is a feeling
of fiery intoxication distilled out of their mutual guilt. In a passage
reminiscent of the forest scene in *The Scarlet Letter*, Miriam urges
Donatello to fling the past behind him. "Forget it! Cast it all behind you," she urges. "The deed has done its office, and has no
existence any more." But it soon becomes apparent that the specter
of guilt is not buried this easily. Donatello, like the fallen Adam,
now repels the woman. He returns to his parental home to make
that agonizing reappraisal of his own heritage which is one of the
first consequences of the union between man and woman. He has
lost his unity with nature; Miriam has lost her friendship with
Hilda.

Like Dimmesdale, Donatello now finds it necessary to avoid men's eyes; he contemplates turning inward to a monkish cell; he is overwhelmed by an exaggerated sense of the past. But he has developed a new dignity, so that his title, the Count of Monte Beni, now seems a more appropriate name. Here in his native land, he and Kenyon educate each other, the sculptor attempting to clarify the Count's muddled thoughts after his shock of recognition, and the Count implicitly demonstrating to Kenyon the difference between vital involvement with the past and mere intellectual apprehension of it. The whole process of moral growth reveals itself to Kenyon from Donatello's tower, as he gazes out over the valley (VI, 297).

> What made the valley look still wider was the two or three varieties of weather that were visible on its surface, all at the same instant of time. Here lay the quiet sunshine; there fell the great black patches of ominous shadow from the clouds; and behind them, like a giant of league-long strides, came hurrying the thunderstorm, which had already swept midway across the plain. In the rear of the approaching tempest, brightened forth again the sunny splendor, which its progress had darkened with so terrible a frown.

The Count's great danger now, as his guide points out, is that he will be hypnotized by the vision of evil. Like Vergil advising Dante in Canto XXX of the *Inferno*, Kenyon tells Donatello that "it was needful for you to pass through that dark valley, but it is infinitely dangerous to linger there too long; there is poison in the atmosphere, when we sit down and brood in it!" (VI, 315). Though he is a wise counselor, Kenyon prefers not to become too deeply involved himself. He watches the process of treading out the wine press; he sees the laborer's feet and garments dyed red as with blood; but he declines a sample of the Tuscan wine. "He had tried a similar draught . . . in years past, and was little inclined to make proof of it again; for he knew that it would be a sour and bitter juice, a wine of woe and tribulation, and that the more a man drinks of such liquor, the sorrier he is likely to be" (VI, 317).

Donatello emerges from the valley and finds blessing when he rejoins Miriam under the statue of Pope Julius. Kenyon's remarks on their reunion are pontifical—he is, in effect, speaking for the Pope—but they make their point (VI, 370):

> Not for earthly bliss, but for mutual elevation, and encouragement towards a severe and painful life, you take each other's hands.

And if, out of toil, sacrifice, prayer, penitence, and earnest effort towards right things, there comes, at length, a sombre and thoughtful happiness, taste it, and thank Heaven! So that you live not for it,—so that it be wayside flower, springing along a path that leads to higher ends,—it will be Heaven's gracious gift, and a token that it recognizes your union here below.

As the Faun, the original type of man, finds his soul and struggles with it "towards the light of heaven," the heavenly vision is brought down to earth. The incarnation of the Holy Spirit in the Dove is, as most readers have agreed, the most ineffective portion of the book. We do not boggle at the dove symbol in Eliot's *Four Quartets;* and we might accept Hilda in a medieval dream vision, but in fiction she is impossible. She needs to be either more adult or else a child, like Pearl, Ilbrahim, or little Joe in "Ethan Brand." If she must be pictured as an adult, Hilda ought to be an ideal who is merely glimpsed at the end. When Hawthorne brings her out of her tower and involves her in the streets of Rome, we expect her to be more human than she can possibly be if she is to retain her allegorical function as spiritual purity. "It is like flinging a block of marble up into the air, and, by some trick of enchantment, causing it to stick there. You feel that it ought to come down, and are dissatisfied that it does not obey the natural law." This is Kenyon's observation about the timeless repose of marble, but it fits the problem of Hilda perfectly. She is associated throughout with the purity of marble. Even the marble image of her hand—the birthmark, the earthly part of Hilda that is all Kenyon can grasp—assumes its share of her remote divinity. Hawthorne apparently expected the reader to sense her icy rigidity and yet to sympathize with her. Thus he is forced into the excessive sentiment of such statements as "Poor sufferer for another's sin."

Nevertheless, this portion of the book has its high points: the description of Sodoma's Christ, with its parallel to Hilda's utter isolation in her vicarious atonement; her reaction to St. Peter's Cathedral; and, above all, her confession to the priest. As she yearns for the relief of the confessional, she sees the inscription '*Pro Anglica Lingua.*' It is "the word in season"; it is Hilda's opportunity to become part of the time-burdened human race; and here, for once, she is "softened out of the chillness of her virgin pride." That Hawthorne intended her to be delicately transformed into a woman from this point onward is clear when Kenyon finds the Venus Donatello has already unearthed. "What is discovery is here," he says. "I seek for Hilda, and find a marble woman! Is the omen good or ill?" The fact that the Venus is "slightly corroded" should supply his answer. But Hilda's purity is never more apparent and never more repulsive than it is in the final scenes with Kenyon.

Part of this is Kenyon's fault. If he is more substantial than Miles Coverdale, he is also much more stuffy. Hawthorne undoubtedly intended to portray the rigidity of the refined intellectual, but surely he did not mean Kenyon to be as insufferable as the modern reader finds him. It is impossible to believe that the man of marble could create a vital statue of Cleopatra. We wonder with Miriam: "Where did you get that secret? You never found it in your gentle Hilda." Kenyon does become slightly more human when Hilda disappears and he wanders in his labyrinth, the streets of Rome. And even he is swept into the swirling movement of the magnificent Carnival scene, as the seven-foot Eve covers him with lime dust. But his final union with Hilda, which should presumably result from a full comprehension of the whole experience, actually amounts to a retreat from it.

Both Hilda and Kenyon, therefore, convince us of the loss that occurs in refinement. Kenyon, who apparently but not convincingly has earlier suffered through a tragic experience, is now content to distill life in his art and in his Hilda, who has her refined sculptor and her religion, which, like her art, is borrowed. Both ultimately remain spectators of the central experience of the book: the wedding of ultimate innocence—Etruria and the living Faun—with all time and all evil—Miriam and Rome.

Thus we are returned to the problem that has provoked much discussion: Does Hawthorne accept or reject the idea of the Fortunate Fall? Miriam, it will be recalled, offers this summary of the Romance:

> The story of the fall of man! Is it not repeated in our romance of Monte Beni? And may we follow the analogy yet further? Was that very sin,—into which Adam precipitated himself and all his race,—was it the destined means by which, over a long pathway of toil and sorrow, we are to attain a higher, brighter, and profounder happiness, than our lost birthright gave? Will not this idea account for the permitted existence of sin, as no other theory can?

Kenyon retreats from her speculation at the time but repeats it a little later for Hilda's consideration. She, in turn, shrinks from the heretical doctrine and convinces Kenyon that this creed makes a mockery of religion and morality. What, then, was Hawthorne's position?

Hyatt H. Waggoner, in the most recent and detailed discussion of this problem, points out the logical implications of the Fortunate Fall: [4]

> Adam's sin, so the argument runs, was the necessary means to man's final salvation, for if he had not sinned, Christ would not have needed to come and we would not know our present hope of glory. Just so, the reasoning was sometimes continued, each one of the elect repeats Adam's history, "sinning" for the greater glory of God and in his own salvation. However one takes it, then, it is at least clear that sin is only good in disguise. In the rather secularized version of the idea presented in *The Marble Faun,* it is a necessary part of our education, a stepping stone to higher things. It is of course an apparently logical deduction from this that man should welcome and perhaps positively seek sin in order to cooperate with Providence.

As his tone would indicate, Waggoner then concludes that "there is every reason to believe that such a line of reasoning seemed to Hawthorne, as it did to Hilda, to make a 'mockery' of religious doctrine and moral law."

Once he has taken this position, however, Waggoner is forced to make a distinction between the meaning Hawthorne "intended" and the one he "achieved." For almost every page of the book indicates that without sin and suffering, moral growth rarely, if ever, results. With the examples of Miriam and Donatello fresh in our minds, it is difficult to see how any other interpretation is possible. Donatello is plunged "into those dark caverns, into which all men must descend, if they would know anything beneath the superficial and illusive pleasures of existence. And when they emerge, though dazzled and blinded by the first glare of daylight, they take truer and sadder views of life forever afterwards." Every human life, if it ascends to truth or delves down to reality, must undergo a similar change" (VI, 302). This progression is presented historically, with the glimpse back into the Golden Age, "before mankind was burdened with sin and sorrow, and before pleasure had been darkened with those shadows that bring it into high relief, and make it happiness" (VI, 104). It is presented scenically,

---

[4] Waggoner, *Hawthorne,* p. 219.

when Kenyon beholds the sunshine, the shadow, the tempest, and
finally the sunny splendor (VI, 297). And, as we have already
seen, it is presented dramatically.

How, then, can so acute a critic as Waggoner argue that Hawthorne did not intend this meaning? Surely Waggoner is right
when he says that Hawthorne, with Hilda, would reject the "line
of reasoning" that is implied in the phrase "the Fortunate Fall."
But he is just as surely wrong in saying that the narrative embodiment of the idea of redemption through sin is confined to Miriam;
that she runs away with the book so that the achieved meaning
differs from the intended meaning. The point is that Hawthorne
and Hilda reject Kenyon's argument precisely because it is a line
of reasoning. Take the narrative element out of the Christian story;
make a logical formula (the Fortunate Fall) of it; remove the
temporal lag between Adam's sin and Christ's redemption and it
becomes a frozen creed that is at best a paradox, at worst a mockery of true morality. We recall that one of the main points of *The
Scarlet Letter* was that moral truth must be apprehended as a
narrative, a parable, an allegory—not as a line of reasoning. This
of course, is only another way of expressing what Christians mean
when they speak of "living by Christ." It is what Hawthorne
meant when he found theological libraries to be a "stupendous
impertinence."

The foregoing discussion prompts a final caution. The Biblical
allusions in Hawthorne's work should not tempt us into reading
it as scripture or theology. The Biblical tongues of flame enabled
the apostles to preach orthodoxy, but in *The Scarlet Letter* Hawthorne shaped his own interpretation of the passage in Acts as he
also formed his own religion. In that book Dimmesdale is in the
church, while Hester remains outside of it; and in *The Marble
Faun* the only religious edifice large enough to hold the characters
at the end is the Pantheon. Hawthorne's position, to use R. W. B.
Lewis' phrase, was an offbeat traditionalism. His emphasis was not
so much upon God's grace as it was upon man's struggle to achieve
it. And ultimately the only way to come at his "religion" is to return to the living letter of his romances.

In Hawthorne's view no automatic formula suffices for meeting
problems of the spirit. In this imperfect world some rise by sin
and some fall by virtue. "Sometimes the instruction comes without
the sorrow," but Hawthorne is dubious about this possibility.
"Oftener the sorrow teaches no lesson that abides with us" (VI,
302). Dimmesdale ascends as a consequence of his sin; Young

Goodman Brown's dying hour is gloom. Like Dimmesdale, Donatello rises spiritually and intellectually, although his flesh is incarcerated; Ethan Brand plunges into the pit. In order to develop his full human potential, man must become fully involved with time yet retain his unique ability to stand aside from its fleeting onrush and contemplate the eternal. This is the tragic vision of Hawthorne's fiction.